SUCCESS IN
THE DIGITAL ECONOMY

How to Overcome Chaos and Create Wealth During Turbulent Times

Nalini Bharkhada

10-10-10
Publishing

SUCCESS IN THE DIGITAL ECONOMY:
How to Overcome Chaos and Create Wealth in Turbulent Times
www.SuccessInTheDigitalEconomyNow.com
Copyright © 2022 Nalini Bharkhada

Paperback ISBN: 978-1-77277-519-8

References to internet websites (URLs) were accurate at the time of writing. Authors and the publishers are not responsible for URLs that may have expired or changed since the manuscript was prepared.

Limits of Liability and Disclaimer of Warranty
The author and publisher shall not be liable for your misuse of the enclosed material. This book is strictly for informational and educational purposes only.

Warning – Disclaimer
The purpose of this book is to educate and entertain. The author and/or publisher do not guarantee that anyone following these techniques, suggestions, tips, ideas, or strategies will become successful. The author and/or publisher shall have neither liability nor responsibility to anyone with respect to any loss or damage caused, or alleged to be caused, directly or indirectly by the information contained in this book.

Publisher
10-10-10 Publishing
Markham, ON   Canada

Printed in Canada and the United States of America

I dedicate this book to you, my dear reader.
It is my sincere intention in writing this book to help you
achieve your ultimate success, wealth and happiness.

To Humanity
May the era of humanism dawn in the world.

Table of Contents

Foreword

Do you want to be successful and wealthy, and enjoy an ideal, happy, peaceful and contented life? Are you healthy and working towards your life's purpose? Do you enjoy fulfilling relationships at work and at home, or are you spending your time running faster, trying to keep up, yet falling further away from living the life that you long for?

Nalini Bharkhada is a successful accountant, entrepreneur, teacher and now an author, and she shares with you her secret about how she used eight simple principles she calls SIMPLIFY, which she put together through her daily practice of self-reflection and finding what works to help make you successful, happy, healthy and wealthy, and build wonderful relationships for a comfortable life.

This book about success in the digital economy, and how to overcome chaos and create wealth during turbulent times, is motivational and inspiring. It will teach you how to work with the universal laws of success to receive the lavish abundance of the universe by simply giving in the areas where you want abundance. This will activate your potentiality, and the actions you take in giving will create the effect of good karma, so that you effortlessly achieve the outcome you are looking for. Through the practice of meditation and detachment, you will discover the purpose of your life. You will start to express your unique talents, fulfill the needs of your fellow humans, and begin to create whatever you want, whenever you want. You will become joyful and carefree, and your life will become an expression of unbounded love and success, no matter how chaotic your external environment is.

SIMPLIFY refers to the eight principles of life, which will teach you to strengthen your relationships, increase your self-esteem and confidence, tackle daily challenges, follow healthy habits, discover your true potential, and live with a passion and purpose, do well at work, realize all your desires and ambitions, and give back to the world.

This marvelous book is a must read, and will teach you how to have success and wealth now, and continue to enjoy it in the future. You will learn that achieving happiness and success is simple and easy. Enjoy!

Raymond Aaron
New York Times **Bestselling Author**

Acknowledgements

I would like to express my heartfelt thanks and gratitude to:

Mahesh, my husband for being my love and best friend. I am extremely grateful for our sacred and rare connection. Thank you for being an incredible rock of support.

My children Dr. Raj, Dr. Neil-Niranjan and Dr. Shreya for their love. I am blessed to be their mother. I am very happy and grateful for my granddaughter Anaya, my little bundle of love and joy.

My parents, now departed, Madhu and Kanchi for their unconditional love and support and teaching me to pursue my dreams with courage and passion.

My parents-in-law, now departed, Pragji and Iccha for their love and support.

Vijay Bhagwat, CA, who taught me meditation and the true meaning of life.

Ramana Rayavarapu, Senior Vice President & BU Leader and Joey Mitchell, Vice President & SBU Controller, for their support while I wrote this book.

For bonuses go to ...

Raymond Aaron and his team for their guidance and support in writing the book.

Cora Cristobal, CPA who is a realtor and real estate investor actively investing in US real estate for introducing me to Raymond Aaron, whose guidance was necessary to write this book.

Sailesh Vaghela, Dinesh Shikotra and Vasant Makwana, for their assistance with the water development projects in East Africa.

Chapter 1
Digital Economy

"The digital economy is impacting us in a big way."
— Cathy Engelbert

What is the Digital Economy?

Digital economy refers to an economy that is based on digital computing technologies, although it is increasingly perceived as conducting business through markets based on the internet and the World Wide Web. The digital economy is also sometimes called the Internet Economy, New Economy, or Web Economy. It's the economic activity that results from billions of everyday online connections among people, businesses, devices, data, and processes. The backbone of the digital economy is hyper-connectivity, which means growing interconnectedness of people, organisations, and machines that results from the Internet, mobile technology and the internet of things (IoT). The Digital Economy is worth more than three trillion dollars today. What is impressive is the fact that this entire value has been generated in the past 20 years since the launch of the Internet. In addition, since Covid-19 has hit us, the digital economy has exploded.

The digital economy is revolutionizing the world of work, making it necessary for businesses to adapt. The driving force of this revolution over the last 20 years has been a 98% reduction in the cost of computing and Internet Connections, driven by technology upgrades that get more powerful. And these trends are expected to accelerate. The business world has been anticipating and planning for the digital age and its impact for the past two decades. However, it is only more recently that we have started seeing how revolutionary these changes may in fact be. In some ways, these new technologies are letting us do the work we have always done, only faster, sometimes better and from different locations. This change with the digital age is not just a cyclical change that will somehow correct itself. We are living in the age of deep and pervasive structural change—the kind where there is no going back. Embracing and leveraging it can accelerate your success.

The digital economy is taking shape and undermining conventional notions about how businesses are structured; how firms interact; and how consumers obtain services, information, and goods. The aggressive use of data is transforming business models, facilitating new products and services, creating new processes, generating greater utility, and ushering in a new culture of management. As an example, Uber, the world's largest taxi company, owns no vehicles. Facebook, the world's most popular media owner, creates no content. Alibaba, the most valuable retailer, has no inventory. And, Airbnb, the world's largest accommodation provider, owns no real estate. Something interesting is happening. These companies have re-imagined the traditional boundaries and value proposition of their industries.

New technologies such as robotics, nano-technologies, self-driving cars—known as exponential technologies that merge the digital world into the physical world —will enable us to enjoy more abundance by generating more breakthroughs in the next two decades than we have ever experienced. Cloud computing and cloud storage is a major paradigm shift for our time; it has become a major time-saver and a safety feature for millions of people. Instead of storing your files on a desktop or laptop computer, cloud storage lets you store your documents, photos, apps and movies, finding space for them, and has become a total storage solution for companies and individuals alike. Files uploaded to the cloud can be accessed anytime from anywhere as long as you have an internet connection.

However, these new technologies are also replacing existing ways of working altogether, and nearly one in 10 jobs is at risk of automation. Job losses are already occurring. Foxconn Technology Group, a manufacturing company that supplies both Apple and Samsung, replaced 60,000 workers with robots. In addition, it is not only the so-called "blue collar" jobs that are affected. Artificial intelligence, or AI, systems are getting increasingly better at specialized tasks such as reading radiology images, making financial trades, and even writing news articles. We do not know exactly what the future holds, but some key changes were already clear pre-Covid-19.

Key Changes Pre-Covid-19

Firstly, as more routine work is automated, workers are expected to do more non-routine work. For example, companies are upgrading their technologies and automating their reports production and dashboards; therefore, employees are no longer required to do these routine tasks but instead are required to provide non-routine tasks of analyzing and interpreting the information available on the dashboards. Similarly, at some fast food chains, machines are already taking orders and handling payments. However, while employees are no longer needed for this type of service, they are needed to handle customers' queries and complaints, and troubleshoot issues with the machines—non-routine tasks that require judgment, critical thinking, and problem-solving.

A second key change is the need to learn and actively engage with new technologies. Increasingly, people in most fields need to work closely with machines and computerized systems, whatever their service or industry. Continued employment means adapting, learning, and using new digital tools as they become increasingly prevalent. More and more, companies are looking to employ people who can embrace new technologies and see them as exciting and valuable tools for success.

This goes hand-in-hand with a third key change: the transition from permanent, office-based jobs to short-term contracts —the so-called "gig" economy. According to one estimate, by the year 2022, two-thirds of all work that organizations do will be project-based, leading to more work being outsourced and done remotely. The digital economy puts pressure on companies to be agile by scaling teams, and their general workforce, up or down as conditions change. In this gig economy, many people switch jobs and careers, and frequently do freelance work. They market themselves to compete for short-term contracts, which require relevant, in-demand skills. As a result, it is becoming less relevant to train for a single vocation; instead, the emphasis is on increasing the ability to learn and master new skills quickly and effectively.

This leads to a fourth key change. With technologies and job roles quickly changing and evolving, skills rapidly become obsolete. This means half of what you learned just five years ago is likely already obsolete. This applies especially in tech-related fields, but it is also increasingly relevant in marketing, sales, manufacturing, law, finance, and much of the rest of the working world.

A fifth key change is that most work today requires greater collaboration and teamwork than in past generations. With more project-based work, individuals need to collaborate more—in many cases, with remote, geographically distributed team members.

Digital tools have expanded the potential for this online collaboration, and companies are using them for a wide range of purposes, from solving problems to engaging with customers and making supply chains more efficient. All of these key changes were already happening pre-Covid-19, and they pointed to one clear shift: that working individuals have to be flexible and update their skills, continuously learning and adapting to stay relevant in the digital economy.

Covid-19 Crisis

With all the changes and disruptions we were already facing in the digital economy, Friday March 13th 2020 came along, when most places around the world announced lockdowns or were getting ready to announce such measures due to the arrival of the virus Covid-19 and the threat of its insidious spread from human to human.

The coronavirus Covid-19 pandemic is the defining global health crisis of our time and the greatest challenge we have faced since World War Two. The virus has created devastating social, economic and political crises that will leave deep scars. We are in uncharted territory. Many of our communities are now unrecognizable. Dozens of the world's greatest cities were deserted as people stayed indoors, either by choice or by government order. Across the world, shops, theatres, restaurants and bars were closed. Schools, universities, and colleges closed either on a nationwide or local basis in many countries affecting approximately 98.5 percent of the world's student population.

Every day, people were losing jobs and income, with no way of knowing when normality would return. Though for many, it was business as usual, as they continued to work out of home, for the others who have lost their jobs or businesses it has caused a huge disruption in their lives.

The Relationship Between Covid-19 and the Digital Economy

The digital economy was already creating a disruption pre-Covid-19. Now it has just quadrupled. Everything is now working on the digital economy. Banking, e-commerce, entertainment streaming, education, consulting, finance & accounting is done online using workplace digital technologies to collaborate, communicate and connect to get the work done. These ranges from HR applications and core business applications to e-mail, instant messaging and enterprise social media tools and virtual meeting tools. The world changed overnight. What the digital economy could not do in 2 years to bring about the digital transformation, Covid-19 has managed to do within a matter of 2 weeks.

The ascendancy of online shopping

Many of us have been shopping online for a long time, buying everything from food to fashion. That shift in shopping behaviour was a major blow to the suburban malls and big box stores. For a while, during Covid time, any outlet that was not selling food and essential home or medical supplies was closed. So nearly, everyone who can shop online has been doing so. If these brick-and-mortar retailers survive the Covid crisis, will they reopen as they were?

The end of cash

Since March 11th 2020, when the World Health Organization declared the outbreak a pandemic, many places are refusing to take coins or bills to avoid touching and have physical contact with the surface touched by somebody else. This begs the question—if we cannot use cash in crisis, do we need cash in normal times? In addition, digital cash is coming, which is different from a credit or debit card that accesses the bank's computer system. It is actual cash on your phone or other digital wallet that moves directly to a merchant, without taking days to "clear & settle." It is faster and cheaper to transact. Cryptocurrencies may displace the US dollar as the world's reserve currency.

The shift to online services and entertainment

Social hotspots such as bars, restaurants and coffee shops, theatres, music venues and sports arenas have been forced to close due to government lockdown so people have taken to gathering online, simultaneously streaming movies and chatting via mobile apps and over social media. If these physical social spaces survive, will they reopen as they were? Will the people be happy gathering online? Will this be the new norm?

The triumph of online education

With schools and universities closed, with no certain date in mind to reopen, teachers turned to deliver courses online. The cost of education would be lower. It avoids physical contact with others. Once delivering courses online is successful, will academic institutions return to what they were doing in physical classrooms or will they continue with delivering online courses or will it be hybrid—partially online and partially in physical classrooms? Will the academic institutions be able to survive without the student fees collected, especially from the international students?

Digital workplace

Working from home works for those in white-collar jobs with privacy, high-speed connectivity and space for all the necessary equipment. It saves a lot of commuting time and may reduce our carbon footprint.

There would be a permanent change in the way business is conducted not only for those who commute by car, but air travel, too. It will take years for business travellers to recover from the PTSD (post-traumatic stress disorder) of Covid-19 and with the rise of online meetings, conferences and collaboration, business air travel will never return to the pre-Covid peaks.

The Future Post Covid-19

The pandemic has completely changed how many of us live and work and some of these changes may be permanent. Organizations will require the flexibility to shape and shift to the new reality. The robots are coming big time—driverless cars, robots in factories and grocery stores, and inventions we have never imagined or thought about. Advances in transportation, medicine, space, and oceanic exploration will have us riveted by continual changes in high technology. This will upend many jobs, and the government will need to institute a massive re-education plan so workers will have another job to go to, using the talents they developed in their years of experience. As organizations journey from responding to the crisis to exploiting opportunities and on to driving growth, they must focus on the three main areas:

People centric

People are the most precious assets and many of them are now working remotely, across all areas of the business ecosystem. They cannot function without digitized processes in a secure, trusted mode.

People may work individually or in team. Opportunities will be available where people's behaviours, experience and privacy will be combined with technology advances. In response to the pandemic, organizations are deploying additional behaviour intelligence at a faster pace.

Location independence

The pandemic has greatly increased the need for location independence. New ways of working mean that employees, customers, suppliers and everyone across the business ecosystem can be located anywhere. Location independence theme will need to address the technology shifts that are driving a distributed cloud structure that facilitates operations anywhere in both business and IT. This theme also describes how a cybersecurity mesh shifts the security perimeter to the individual.

Resilient delivery

This theme is not about "bouncing back"— it is about having the ability to nimbly adapt in a dynamic business environment. The theme's underlying assumption is that volatility exists, so it is vital to have the skills, capabilities, techniques, operational processes and systems to constantly adapt to changing patterns. This also means organizations must be composed, with modular, adjustable, autonomous components. They must use sophisticated technologies such as AI, engineering the approach with a disciplined focus to achieve sustained resiliency. In addition, business and IT processes must be automated, hence the relentless zeal for hyper-automation.

Global Responsibility

The pandemic has taught us that we are all connected and inter-dependent. Someone gets a new virus in Asia and 3 months later, the global economy shuts down. Alternatively, if one person does not act in a socially responsible way during a pandemic, they can affect the future of the entire world. Our *local* actions can have *global* consequences. Today in the smaller world, when we act, we "act global." We are all facing the biggest crisis since the Second World War and we need global solutions to these global problems. Is a deeper understanding of the danger of climate change next? The stronger trend will be that we live on this planet together.

The economic costs of Covid-19 are devastating, on a scale perhaps never seen in modern history. The human costs are at this stage, unfathomable. This is one of those rare turning points in history. The Covid-19 pandemic will cause profound changes to our economy, our behaviour and society locally as well as globally. Some leaders and governments that failed the challenges will be replaced. Many institutions will be scrutinized and changed for the better.

When all this ends—and it will, the way we perform our jobs, entertain ourselves and go about our daily lives could see a dramatic change for the better. We could become better global citizens, more interested in the news and political choices, more self-involved, more family oriented and more appreciative of life.

More than before pre-Covid-19 times, the digital arena is now even more chaotic and turbulent with uncertainty over work, economy, education and health. With talks about reopening the economy, there is further uncertainty regarding how safe is it to go to work, or to go out to the restaurants or movies or even to the park. The world has changed forever and until everyone is vaccinated to protect them against the virus, the fear of catching the virus will be topmost on everyone's mind when around people. The companies will also face the dilemma of ensuring the workplace is safe.

In this type of chaotic environment during these turbulent times, how can one be successful or remain successful? How can you overcome the chaos and create wealth during these turbulent times. Most people have not faced such circumstances in their lifetimes before. Neither have I. However, one thing is certain. There have been such times in history before, where the circumstances and laws under which we operated under then and now are not much different, and if we had success then, we will certainly have success now and going forward as well.

In the next chapter, I will talk about what these laws are under which we were governed and operated in the past. These same laws still exist and govern us today, and always will in the future till eternity. As the world goes into more disruption, we need to understand these laws and operate under them accordingly so that we can continue to create wealth and be successful always.

Chapter 2
The Laws of
Nature and Success

"Happiness is when what you think,
what you say, and what you do are in harmony."
— Mahatma Gandhi

Success means different things to different people. Having material abundance certainly makes the journey of life more enjoyable but it is not the only component of success. Having excellent health, energy, zest or enthusiasm for life, fulfilling relationships and freedom are equally important to have success. What is the use of having plenty of wealth or money but not being healthy to be able to enjoy this money with your loved ones, or enjoy life? Success is the ability to fulfill your desires with effortless ease, yet many consider success including creation of wealth to be hard work, and often at the expense of others.

To me success means having peace, happiness and contentment with whatever I have. It is the progressive realization of worthy goals and being at peace with having achieved these goals. It is being increasingly happy and content with what we have achieved so far. The happiness awakens the divinity within you and you will see divinity everywhere around you—in the beauty of a flower, flight of a bird, or in the eyes of a child. Then you will experience magic and miracles, and when this happens not occasionally but all the time—that is the true meaning of success.

So when my clients ask me how they can experience this expression of divinity and achieve this true meaning of success, I tell them that they need to first understand the universal laws of nature and success that everyone is governed by and has operated under for eons. If they abide by these laws, they will achieve the true meaning of success, effortlessly and with ease. If they violate these laws, they will pay the price in accordance to the degree of violation.

So what are these laws of nature and success?

They are also referred to as laws of Life. They are the same principles that nature uses to create everything in material existence— everything that we can see, hear, smell, taste or touch. It is similar to laws and regulations of a corporation—what we call Corporate Code of Conduct where a corporation will list out all the rules they want the employees or members of the organization to follow. As an example, all organizations expect their members and employees to act with integrity and to treat each other with respect. Anyone who violates these rules would face the consequences and might even be asked to leave the company.

Similarly, the laws of nature and success listed below are the laws which govern us and we have to abide by, for living in this universe. If we violate them, we would face the consequences. However, if we work in harmony with them, we will create wealth and success with care-freeness, joy and love. Incorporating the knowledge of these laws in our consciousness, and then working in harmony with them, will give us the ability to create unlimited wealth with effortless ease, and to experience success in every endeavour we undertake, whether it is in digital or mass-production era.

1. The Law of Pure Consciousness. This law is based on the fact that we are in our essential state, pure consciousness or pure potentiality; it is the field of all possibilities and infinite creativity within the bounds and limits of nature. The source of abundance is infinite, and you can create and have anything you want. This field of pure consciousness or potentiality is your own self, the soul. Being infinite and unbounded, it is also pure joy. In addition, the more you experience your true nature, the closer you are to the field of pure consciousness or potentiality. It is completely free of any fear, compulsion to control, and no struggle for approval and external power, unlike your ego, which is your self-image and thrives on approval; it wants to control and is sustained by power, because it lives in fear.

All of material creation, everything that we can see, touch, taste, hear, or smell is made of the same stuff and comes from the same source, Cosmos. Everyone and everything is connected to everyone and everything else. We are all part of the same creation and same collective consciousness. Our physical body, the physical universe— anything and everything that we can perceive through our senses—is the transformation of the un-manifest, unknown and invisible into the manifest, known and visible.

If you want to enjoy the benefits of the field of pure consciousness or potentiality and make full use of the creativity, then you need access to it. Four ways to access this field are:

- Through the daily practice of silence—meaning "Just to be" in the moment. To be "present" and "aware." It quietens your mind and internal dialogue or chatter.

- Through the daily practice of meditation—where you learn to experience the field of pure silence and pure awareness where exists the field of infinite correlation and organizing power, the ultimate ground of creation in the Cosmos where everything is inseparably connected with everything else called the Cosmic Energy.

- Through the daily practice of non-judgement—you are constantly evaluating, classifying, analyzing and labelling that something is good or bad, or right or wrong, then you create a lot of turbulence in your internal dialogue. Non-judgement creates silence in your mind.

- Regularly spending time in nature whether it be a lake, river, forest, a mountain, a stream or the seashore. That connection with nature's intelligence will also help you access the field of pure potentiality. It enables you to sense the harmonious interaction of all the elements and forces of life, and gives you a sense of unity with all of life.

All of the above will give you access to the qualities inherent in the field; infinite creativity, freedom and bliss. As you gain more and more access to your true nature, you will spontaneously receive creative thoughts; because the field of pure potentiality is also field of infinite creativity and pure knowledge.

The lavish display and abundance of the universe is the expression of the creative mind of nature. The more you are tuned in to the mind of the nature, the more you will have access to its infinite, unbounded creativity. But first, you have to go beyond the turbulence of your internal dialogue to connect with that abundant, infinite and creative mind.

2. The Law of Giving and Receiving. The universe operates through dynamic exchange, i.e. giving and receiving, which are different aspects of the flow of the energy in the universe. Nothing is static in the universe. Your body is in a constant exchange with the body of the universe. Your mind is dynamically interacting with the mind of the Cosmos; your energy is the expression of the cosmic energy. Because your body and your mind and the universe are in constant and dynamic exchange, stopping the circulation of energy is like stopping the flow of good things in your life. This is why you must give in order to receive, to keep wealth and affluence in your life.

Every relationship is also one of give and take, and in reality receiving is the same as giving, because giving and receiving are different aspects of the flow of energy in the universe. If you interfere with the flow of either, you interfere with the nature's intelligence. The more you give, the more you will receive, because you will keep the abundance of the universe circulating in your life. Anything of value in life only multiplies when given. If you give grudgingly and feel you have lost something, then the increase will not happen, as there is no energy behind that giving.

It is the intention behind your giving and receiving that is the most important thing. The intention should always be to create happiness for the giver and receiver, and this will therefore generate increase. The return is directly proportional to the giving when it is unconditional and from the heart. The act of giving has to be joyful. Then the energy behind the giving increases many times over.

So this law is very simple: if you want joy, give joy to others; if you want love, learn to give love; if you want wealth, help others to become wealthy; if you want attention and appreciation, learn to give attention and appreciation. The easiest way to get what you want is to help others get what they want. This principle works equally well for individuals, corporations, societies and nations. In recent years, corporations are focusing on corporate social responsibility activities, which helps to improve the company's image, and attracts customers and investors who have same values and build the company's brand. Some companies like Facebook and Google, who provided free services, have done extremely well and earn high returns.

3. The Law of Cause and Effect. It is also known as law of karma or "We reap what we sow" or "What goes around comes around." Whatever you send out into the universe comes back. In physics courses, we learnt that "action and re-action are equal and opposite." Karma is both action and the consequence of that action; it is cause and effect simultaneously. If we want to create happiness in our lives, we must learn to sow the seeds of happiness. Karma implies the action of conscious choice making. Some of these choices are made consciously and others unconsciously. Everything that happens is a result of the choices we have made in the past, whether consciously or unconsciously. When making a choice, ask yourself if the choice you make brings happiness to you as well as to others around you who are influenced by your choice. If so, then go ahead and make the choice. If it brings distress to you or those around you, then do not make that choice. There is only one choice, out of an infinity of choices available, that will create happiness for you as well as for others around you.

The universe has an interesting mechanism to help us make the correct choice at any given time. It has to do with the sensations we experience in our body—one is a sensation of comfort and the other is a sensation of discomfort. When you make the choice consciously and the body sends you a sensation of comfort, then you have made the right choice. If the body sends you a message of discomfort, then it is not an appropriate choice.

You need to understand that based on this law, your future is generated by the choices you make today. Under the law of karma, no debt goes unpaid. There is a perfect accounting system in the universe, so either you pay the karmic debt, even if a lot of suffering is involved in the payment of the debt, or you transform your debt to a desirable experience and ask yourself what I can learn from this experience so you do not make the same mistake again. Then share the lesson with others so they do not make the same mistake. This way you have converted your karmic debt to bring a benefit to others. In this case, you still pay your debt but you are able to take a karmic episode and create a new and positive karma out of it by sharing your learning with others so they can benefit and not make the same mistake.

4. The Law of Least Effort. This law is based on the fact that nature's intelligence functions with effortless ease and care-freeness. This is the principle of least action, of no resistance, i.e. the principle of harmony and love. When we learn this lesson from the nature, we easily fulfill our desires. In nature, you will observe that least effort is expended. Grass does not try to grow, it just grows. Flowers do not try to bloom, they just bloom. Birds and fish do not try to fly or swim, they just fly and swim. This is their intrinsic nature. It is the nature of the sun to shine and stars to glitter and sparkle. In addition, it is human nature to make our dreams manifest into physical form, easily and effortlessly. This means that you have a faint idea, and then the manifestation of the idea comes about effortlessly. What is commonly called a 'miracle' is actually an expression of the law of least effort.

When you are in harmony with nature, when you have the knowledge of your true Self, then you can make use of the law of least effort. Least effort is expended when your actions are motivated by love, because nature is held together by the energy of love. When you seek power and control over other people, you waste energy. When you seek money or power for the sake of the ego, you spend energy chasing an illusion of happiness instead of enjoying happiness in the moment. When you seek money for personal gain only, you cut off the flow of energy to yourself, and interfere with the expression of nature's intelligence. However, when your actions are motivated by love, then your energy multiplies and accumulates—and the surplus energy you gather and enjoy can be channelled to create anything that you want, including unlimited wealth.

For law of least effort to work, first you have to **accept** people, situations, circumstances and events as they occur and not as you wish. When you do this, you are ready to accept **responsibility** for your situation and for all the events, you see as a problem i.e. you do not blame anyone or anything for your situation, including yourself. Now you have the ability to have a creative response to the situation as it is. Next is **defencelessness**, which means that you have relinquished the need to convince or persuade others of your point of view. If you stop fighting and resisting, you will fully experience the present, which is a gift. The past is history, the future is a mystery, and this moment is a gift. That is why this moment is called 'the present.'

5. The Law of Intention and Desire. This law is based on the fact that energy and information exists everywhere in nature and in the quantum field of pure consciousness or pure potentiality. In addition, this quantum field is influenced by intention and desire. Your body is not separate from the body of the universe, because at quantum mechanical levels there are no well-defined edges. You are like a wiggle, a wave or a fluctuation in the larger quantum field—the universe—which is your extended body.

We are a privileged species in that we have a human nervous system capable of becoming aware of the information and energy of our own quantum field, and because human consciousness is infinitely flexible through this wonderful nervous system, we are able to consciously change the informational content that gives rise to our physical body. You can consciously change the energy and informational content of your own body, and therefore influence the energy and informational content of your extended body—your environment, your world—and cause things to manifest in it.

This conscious change is brought about by the two qualities inherent in consciousness, attention and intention. Attention energizes, and intention transforms. Whatever you put your attention on will grow stronger in your life. Whatever you take your attention away from will disintegrate, wither and disappear. Intention, on the other hand, triggers transformation of energy and information and organizes its own fulfillment.

The quality of intention on the object of attention will orchestrate an infinity of space-time events to bring about the outcome intended, provided one follows the other laws of nature and success. It is the driving force of creation, and through your intent you can literally command the laws of nature to fulfill your dreams and desires. You can put the cosmic computer with its infinite organizing power to work for you. Intention lays the groundwork for the effortless, spontaneous flow of pure potentiality seeking expression from the un-manifest to the manifest. The only caution is that you use your intent for the benefit of humanity. This happens spontaneously when you are in alignment with the seven laws of nature and success.

6. The Law of Detachment. The Law of Detachment says that in order to acquire anything in the physical universe, you have to relinquish your attachment to it. This does not mean you give up the intention to create your desire. You give up your attachment to the result. This is a very powerful thing to do. The moment you relinquish your attachment to the result, combining one-pointed intention with detachment at the same time, you will have that which you desire. Anything you want can be acquired through detachment, because detachment is based on the unquestioning belief in the power of your true Self. Attachment, on the other hand, is based on fear and insecurity—and the need for security is based on not knowing the true Self.

Attachment is always to material things. Detachment is synonymous with wealth consciousness. With detachment there is freedom to create. You have to embrace the wisdom of uncertainty and you will find the freedom to create anything you want. Without uncertainty, there can be no creativity. Uncertainty means stepping into the unknown every moment of our existence. The unknown is the field of all possibilities, ever fresh, ever new, always open to the creation of new manifestations. Without uncertainty and the unknown, life becomes boring and just a collection of outworn memories.

Relinquish your attachment to the known, step into the unknown, and step into the field of all possibilities. This means that in every moment of your life, you will have joy, laughter, excitement, adventure and mystery. You will experience the fun of life—the magic of life where wealth is created, spontaneously and effortlessly. True wealth consciousness is the ability to have anything you want, anytime you want, and with the least effort.

7. The Law of Purpose in Life. We are spiritual beings living in a physical body, and this law says that we have taken manifestation in physical form to fulfill a purpose. According to this law, you have a unique talent and a unique way of expressing it. There is something that you can do better than anyone else in the whole world—and for every unique talent and unique expression of that talent, there are also unique needs. Expressing your talents to fulfill these needs creates unlimited wealth and abundance.

The law of purpose in life says that each of us is here to discover our true Self, i.e. to discover our higher or spiritual self, which is beyond our ego. Secondly, we need to express our unique talents. When you are doing that one thing, you lose track of time. Thirdly, the purpose in life is to provide service to humanity—to serve your fellow human beings and to ask yourself the questions, "How can I help? How can I help all those that I come into contact with?" When you combine the ability to express your unique talent with service to humanity, you make full use of the law of purpose in life. In addition, coupled with the experience of your own spirituality, the field of pure potentiality, there is no way you will not have access to unlimited abundance, because that is the real way abundance is achieved.

This is not the temporary abundance; it is permanent, because of your unique talent, your way of expressing it and your service and dedication to your fellow human beings, which you discover through asking the question, "How can I help? instead of "What's in it for me?" Discover your divinity, find your unique talent, serve humanity with it, and you can generate all the wealth that you want. You will begin to experience your life as a miraculous expression of divinity—not just occasionally, but all the time. In addition, you will know true joy and the true meaning of success

You will notice that all of these laws are interconnected and we need to understand these laws to be healthy, wealthy and happy. The law of pure consciousness or potentiality is activated by the law of giving, and through the actions you take in giving, will activate the law of karma and create good karma. This makes everything in life easy; you don't have to expend a lot of effort to fulfill your desires, and this automatically leads to understanding the law of least effort. When everything happens easily and effortlessly, then it is easy to understand the law of intention and desire, as well as to practise the law of detachment.

Finally, as you begin to understand all of the laws, you will begin to focus on your true purpose in life, leading you to use the law of purpose where you start to express your unique talents, fulfill the needs of your fellow humans, and begin to create whatever you want and whenever you want. You become joyful and carefree, and your life becomes an expression of unbounded love and success, which you can achieve effortlessly no matter how chaotic the environment is.

You will notice that these laws have governed us in the past and these same laws still exist and govern us today, and always will until eternity, whether we operate in mass-production or digital economy. So as long as we operate under these laws and do not violate them, then we will continue to have success and an abundance of wealth no matter how much disruption is going on in our external environment and economy.

In the next chapter, I will talk about daily routines or habits you need to adopt which are self-maintaining and self-enhancing, and lead to a happy, successful, productive and peaceful life.

Chapter 3
Self-Discipline

"Quality is not an act, it is a habit."
— Aristotle

Daily Routines and Habits

To have a full, rich and successful life, you not only need to act in harmony with the Laws of Success, but you also need to have daily routines and good habits which when repeated regularly on a daily basis will translate into massive amounts of peace, happiness, money, confidence, self-esteem and your progress in almost any area of your life. When asked by my clients what I do, I tell them that I use **SIMPLIFY** daily. It is an acronym, which stands for

Self Discipline
Increase in Wealth
Meditation
Purpose
Learn
Invest in Others
Food
Yourself

By practising **SIMPLIFY** daily, you can have massive success and wealth in all areas of your life. By focusing daily on all areas of your life, you will find yourself improving *synergistically* in each area and your life becomes a whole.

I grew up in Kenya on the east coast of Africa, on the island of Mombasa which was inhabited by 2.6 million people. It is a diverse community with many settlers from different parts of the world who settled in Mombasa, all living peacefully together and following their religious beliefs. As a result, there are many churches, mosques and temples on the island. Mombasa had no television until I was in my late teens, though Nairobi, the capital of Kenya, always had television. On the other hand, the island of Mombasa is surrounded by the Indian Ocean and there is a jungle where wild animals such as lions, elephants, giraffes, zebras, leopards, rhinoceros and antelopes live. Therefore, there is plenty to do in connection with nature, and my childhood was busy with school on weekdays and enjoying the nature on weekends and holidays.

Since there was no television in Mombasa, the evenings, usually after a light dinner, included reflecting and reviewing over the day's events, planning for the next day and then settling for the night reading a book. Books provided connection to the outside world, and played an important role in my life. At minimal cost, books allow you to get knowledge about the rest of the world and have great conversations with an author. You might never get to meet in person Warren Buffet or Bill Gates and talk for three hours, but reading a book written by them will enable you to learn how they think, and about their success strategies. It also allows you to recognize your own self-talents and builds your own confidence and self-discipline.

In Mombasa, lunch was a large affair. It was the biggest meal of the day and I looked forward to the daily nap after lunch (siesta time). It did wonders for the digestion of food, and the short nap provided a burst of fresh energy and boosted productivity in the afternoon.

It is always hot, 34 degrees every day, and I lived according to the way of life on the island, following the rituals and hence acquiring some routines which became habits over the years. I also learned many things from observing the wild animals while on a safari. (Safari is a Swahili word for travel. The national language for Kenya is Swahili.)

Self-Discipline

Self-discipline is the ability you have to control and motivate yourself, stay on track and do what is right. It is a learned skill and is the key to reaching your goals, having great success and happiness, and creating a better life.

It is a habit anyone can learn with practice and repetition. Your ability to develop this habit will contribute more to your success than any other quality of character. In order to be successful you have to do what successful people do. Successful people are highly disciplined in the important work they do. Self-disciplined people have the ability to think long term, sacrifice or delay gratification in the short term so that they can enjoy even greater rewards in the long term. The payoff for practising self-discipline is immediate. Whenever you discipline yourself, and force yourself to do the right thing, whether you feel like it or not, you will like and respect yourself more. It avoids having regrets in the future, that though it was the right thing to do, you did not do it. Your self- esteem and confidence increases and your brain releases endorphins, making you happy and proud.

You need to develop a few disciplines if you want to achieve your full potential.

The Discipline of Waking Up Early

As the saying goes, "Early to bed and early to rise makes one healthy, wealthy and wise." Fortunately, I picked up this habit naturally, as no matter where you lived around the town of Mombasa where I grew up, there was a mosque close by. Prayers are done 5 times during the day over loudspeakers, which can be heard all over the town, and the first one starts at 4.30 a.m. This became my natural alarm clock and my wakeup call each morning at 4.30 a.m. The second prayer starts at 5.00 a.m. by which time there is full daylight, the birds start chirping, the crows start crowing and chickens start clucking. It is impossible to sleep with this loud natural music going on and I just jumped out of bed every morning at 5.00 a.m. Then I would get ready and go with my father to a place called "Lighthouse" where we would walk for about 45 minutes in front of the Indian Ocean. The brisk cool air from the sea blowing over my face and body did wonders; it puts you in the right frame of mind to start the day. On our way home after the walk, we stopped at the Shiv temple first, to bow down and say thank you to Almighty.

Just before the sun rises, the timing is known as the "Creator Hours" and there is a lot of cosmic energy present in the universe between 3 a.m. and 6 a.m. During this time most people are asleep, therefore there is no traffic jam of thoughts in nature. This way whatever thoughts you put out will quickly manifest in physical reality and you will find solutions to your problems easily. During the day there is a traffic jam of thoughts as everyone is up and putting out their thoughts, so your thought takes longer to manifest in physical reality. Waking up early and then spending time in solitude, walking in nature, is one single routine that gave me a great start to the day. Whenever you practise solitude for more than thirty minutes, you activate your superconscious mind and trigger your intuition. You get solutions for the issues or problems you are trying to solve from your voice within. In addition, the physical activity of walking releases dopamine, an inspirational neurotransmitter, which regulates mood and muscle movement and is stored in the brain. It explains why you feel energized. Serotonin, which is a pleasure neurotransmitter and makes you feel happy, is also released, which helps regulate mood, body temperature and appetite. The majority of serotonin is stored in the gut instead of the brain. When you feel happy, you are more creative, you have more energy and you feel incredible confidence. It will also increase your metabolic rate, which allows you to burn fat more quickly and reduces your cravings. What a great way to start the day.

When I moved to Canada, I first settled in Montreal and was fortunate to live by the St. Lawrence River, which allowed me to walk by the waterfront every day. After living in Montreal for 20 years, I moved to Toronto, where I missed these walks by the waterfront. Now in summer, I go for a walk for about 15 minutes around the block where I live and in winter, I just walk on the treadmill at home. After getting ready, I do meditation, giving me a perfect start to the day. I review my to-do list I created the day before and start cracking on the important tasks and activities I had planned for the day. This to-do list is an effective way of planning and scheduling. In addition, as the old adage goes, what gets planned and scheduled, gets done.

When you exercise discipline in one area, it strengthens every other discipline at the same time. For example, if you get up at 5.00 a.m. and do some walking and meditation, you will be happy and have more energy to plan and work on your goals and to-do lists. You will manage your time better and accomplish more.

Habits, once formed, are hard to break. This habit of waking up at 5.00 a.m. has stayed with me over the years and until this present day I still wake up at 5.00 a.m. or before. This one single habit has enabled me to focus on myself with no one interrupting and distracting me, inspiring new ideas and solutions and empowering me to make better decisions.

The Discipline of SimbaWalk (small steps)

Simba (Simba is the Swahili word for lion) is called the king of the jungle and is a very strong and powerful animal. It looks magnificent and majestic, and I love watching a team of lions resting under the trees after they have had lunch. They look very calm as compared to seeing them live in the act of hunting for their food. Their roar is ferocious then, and the other animals run for their lives. During the many safaris I have been on, I observed that the lion walks very gracefully. It takes about 15 steps forward then stops, looks to the right then to the left and then proceeds on again. It will take another 15 steps and again looks to the right and then to the left and then proceeds again. Even though it is the king of the jungle, it proceeds cautiously by taking small steps and then looking around to see that no danger is around before proceeding again. Taking small steps and then, taking the time to review has enabled the lion to become the king of the jungle.

I call this way of moving forward, SimbaWalk, i.e. taking a few small steps forward then observing to achieve excellence. I have adopted SimbaWalk by practising it every day and make a list of important things, which I need to accomplish, and then prioritize the list to a few items, which are priority for the day. As items are completed I cross them out and at the end of the day, I review the list to see if I accomplished and completed the items on the list. All items of priority are completed and crossed out, and the remaining ones go back on the list created for the next day. It gives me great pleasure and satisfaction to roll the paper, crunch it into a ball, and toss it in the recycling bin and say, "Done." It avoids procrastination, making you do the task today instead of leaving it for tomorrow, which sometimes never comes. I sometimes make a digital list and then cross out the done items which works equally well.

Taking these small steps brings about small improvements which when done daily and consistently brings about stunning results and at the end of the month, you will observe that you have accomplished huge strides with these daily small steps.

The self-review at the end of the day allows me to see how I have performed versus what I planned, make any improvements if necessary by going back and redoing an activity, or if this is not possible then learning from it so that I will do it better next time. This way you are focused on your priorities and your values, and this builds and enhances your human potential. The Japanese call this 'kaizen' or in other words continuous improvement.

With this one habit, you can accomplish extraordinary things by becoming a tiny bit better each day. By increasing your productivity, performance and output by a small amount each day, say 5 important tasks completed well, then at the end of the week you will have completed 35 tasks and at the end of the month, 150 tasks and at the end of the year, it will be 1,825 tasks and so on.

Since virtually every improvement compounds, like interest, it will affect your other areas of performance at the same time, increasing your value, success and income exponentially.

The Discipline of Hard Work

Another interesting trait, which I learned from the lion, was to work hard. A few times while on a safari, I have watched the lion in action when it was hunting. Contrary to my thinking, the lion has to work extremely hard in order to kill an animal for food. I had thought that the lion, being powerful and the king of the jungle, would be able to catch its prey easily, but that is not true. I have never seen the actual 'kill' nor do I want to as I am sure it is a gruesome scene, but at times I have waited for over an hour watching the lion in action and it has not managed to catch its prey. Losing patience, I have just driven on.

Anders Ericsson at the University of Florida pioneered the 10 Years Rule and found that great performers spend the equivalent of ten years or ten thousand hours practising their skill before the first signs of genius show up. These elite performers each total at least ten thousand hours of practice.

Bill Gates as a young boy spent tens of thousands of hours trying to learn the strange new device, when the first mainframe computer came out. He got opportunities during his high school, summer and where he lived which gave him extra time to practise so that when he started his own software company, he had already been programming practically nonstop for seven consecutive years, which was way past ten thousand hours. How many teenagers in the world had this kind of experience that Bill Gates had? No wonder Bill was considered a genius. It is hours of hard work to achieve anything of significance and importance.

Throughout history, you will notice that whoever has achieved anything lasting and worthwhile, had engaged in long, often unappreciated hours, weeks, months and even years of concentrated, disciplined work, in a particular direction.

Similarly the higher the position one holds, the more power they have, and they work very hard as well. I was the President of three small manufacturing companies in Montreal. These were photo labs. I started with one and then acquired two more at the same time as I started my education in the 2-year Executive MBA program at Concordia University. The first semester had thirteen courses. My two sons at the time were six and four years old. Studying and at the same time raising and looking after my young children, together with completing due diligence and acquiring two new companies and then operating all three companies was insane amounts of work. During the first semester with thirteen courses, I thought the nightmare would never end and I would lose everything. My husband helped as much as he could but he had his own job to work at as well. I was the only one in that entire MBA program who had young children of that age. Besides my husband and children, I had no family in Montreal on whom I could rely for help. Looking back, I do not know how I managed it all. All I can remember is I worked day and night. I worked extremely hard at whatever was a priority, including my family; the rest I delegated to others. I am glad Montreal has many family owned good restaurants as we ate out a lot since there was no time to prepare and cook meals.

At the end of the first semester, I learnt a great lesson. No matter how tough and impossible the situation is, by giving it all you have, making a sincere effort and working hard, you can achieve and do anything you want and be successful.

The Discipline of Time Management

Time management is a central skill of success, and the discipline of good time management spreads to all your other disciplines. It has immediate payoff in improved results, and long-term payoff in terms of the quality of your work. To be successful, you have to be extremely well organized and give an enormous amount of thought as to where you use your time. Time is perishable i.e. you cannot save it. The only thing you can do is allocate it differently, move time away from activities of low value to activities of higher value. Allocate time to the goals and activities that you need to accomplish in terms of priority. The more you plan, the better you use your time and the more you will accomplish. Block time on your calendar for the "Must Do" and important activities. Multi-tasking when doing simple manual tasks is fine, but serious work requires full concentration so discipline yourself so that you concentrate single-mindedly on your important activities until they are 100% complete. Eliminate non-value added activities, complete "Should Do and Nice to Do" activities when there is time, and delegate the rest of the activities.

Time management requires that you do what is difficult and valuable before you do what is fun, easy, and unimportant. The reason time management is so important is that it enables you to control the sequence of events. You choose what you are going to do first, what you are going to do next and what you are not going to do at all. Avoid time wasters and learn to say "no" whenever anyone or anything attempts to take up your time on an activity that is not particularly important or valuable. The happiest people are those that spend time very carefully on only those activities that are important to them.

Distraction from instant messaging and social media plays havoc on one's brain in the long run, as one stops doing one task to respond to another and then switches back and forth. Neural connections are created in the brain while working on a specific task and these get broken when you respond to instant messaging or social media. Another connection is created when you return to the original task and then gets broken again. Over time as one gets older this creating, breaking, creating, and breaking of neural connections in the brain leads to Alzheimer's, digital dementia or what they call "seniors" disease. Some people try to be on top of everything attending to all social media distractions, instant messages and texts and at the same time do their work with no concern for the long-term consequences for the impact on their brains. So allocate your valuable time on your value adding and important tasks.

The Discipline of Courage

The biggest obstacle to success in life is fear of failure, expressed in the feeling that, "I can't do it." If you are human, you are going to face fear. Courage requires that you make yourself do what you should do, that you deal with your fears rather than avoiding them. Courage is a habit, developed by practising courage whenever it is required. As Emerson said, "Do the thing you fear and the death of fear is certain." Make a habit of confronting your fears rather than avoiding them. When you confront the fear and move towards it, especially if it is another person or situation, the fear gets smaller and you become braver. Repeat the words to cancel fear, "I can do it!" over and over, to build up your courage and confidence. Identify one fear in your life and then discipline yourself to deal with it, to confront it, to do whatever it involves, as quickly as you possibly can. The payoff for identifying a fear and confronting it is tremendous; it gives you the courage and confidence to go through your life and deal with every fear-inducing situation.

Developing resilience and hardiness in the face of fear is what leaders do. The things that most frighten us, when we actually have the courage to do them, dissolve. How many times have you been so afraid to do something and finally decide to confront it, running towards it, only to find that the very act of running towards it has dissolved fear itself? Practise courage and you will become fearless. One of the real reasons we do not do the things that frighten us is because we are afraid of being judged. We are afraid of failure. We are afraid of being criticized or ridiculed. We are afraid of not succeeding. We are afraid of stumbling. Many people spend their entire lives holding themselves back from doing what they really want to do because of fears of some kind.

However, if you relinquish the attachment to the outcome and step into the unknown, where lies the field of all possibilities, ever fresh, ever new and always open to the creation of new manifestations, you will develop a sense of fearlessness and a sense of bravery within you. Where the attachment to the outcome created the fear of failing or stumbling, the uncertainty, which is the fertile ground of pure creativity and freedom, will bring on courage. Doing the things that frighten you and not worrying about what happens will eventually make you fearless.

Everything that we now find easy was initially hard. Every master was once a beginner. So be courageous and welcome the difficult task that you need to do. It will be hard in the beginning but as you work on it and begin to understand it, the fear within you will just disappear and you will have a beautiful solution at the end. Your level of confidence will increase. You will become a more powerful person. You can then use your success as a platform for going after even more difficult tasks, and then the rest of your life will be just an exercise in you becoming a courageous and a fearless soul. When you look back, you will then laugh at the fact that what you thought was difficult was very easy. Habits largely determine your future. 95% of everything you do is based on your habits. Being disciplined in the above habits have helped me to move forward in my life. So develop, master and cultivate some good disciplines and habits, which work for you and you can use your full potential and have a successful future. In the next chapter I will talk to you about how you can create an increase in your wealth.

Chapter 4
Increase in Wealth

"Health is the greatest gift, contentment the greatest wealth, faithfulness the best relationship."
— Buddha

Accounting Terms

In purely accounting terms, increase in wealth means either an increase in your income and assets or a decrease in your expenses and liabilities. You need to consciously watch your financial situation on a regular basis to make sure that you are increasing your income and assets and not the other way around, by increasing your expenses and liabilities. The exception is if the liability or expense is for an investment purpose such as buying a house which will increase your liability and expense but at the same time give you an opportunity to live in and enjoy a beautiful place of your choice, and that which will appreciate in value in the future. Alternatively, you could spend money or get a loan to learn something for yourself or for your children. This is an investment where the new learning will enable you to earn more income in the future.

Increase in wealth happens when you:

1. Increase your clients, sales and reduce your debts.
2. Raise your fees or your prices, or sell something you own.
3. Get a credit card, pay off the balance on your credit card, or get rid of a credit card.

4. Buy a property, mortgage or refinance a property, pay down your mortgage.
5. Decrease the interest rate on your debt and increase the interest rate on your savings.
6. Network and improve your referral system.
7. Get a promotion and a raise if you are employed.
8. Buy stocks or mutual funds.

All of the above steps, if done continuously on a consistent basis, will improve your financial situation and your wealth.

During the pandemic, you needed to carefully think about where you were going to spend your money. The stimulus in trillions of US dollars injected into the global economy in a very short period, and with interest rates close to zero, turned every investment class into a bubble. Many assets value have spiralled upwards in less than a year and Bitcoin, the largest of the world's more than 4000 cryptocurrencies crossed $50,000(US) which is a nine-fold increase in the price of Bitcoin in the short eleven months since the outset of the pandemic before it crashed. So many of the investments are overvalued and poised to crash. During this time, the thing to do with your hard earned money is to safeguard it until the danger of the health and economic crisis has passed.

Money is good. It takes money to buy homes, cars, food, clothes and most of the good things in life, which makes the journey in life more comfortable. Money has an energy of its own and is largely attracted to people who are good with it and who treat it well. It tends to flow towards those people who can use it in the most productive ways to produce goods and services and to create employment and opportunities that benefit others. At the same time, money flows away from those who use it poorly or who spend it in non-productive ways.

In fact, money is very much like a lover. It must be courted, coaxed, flattered, and treated with care and attention. It gravitates towards people who respect it, value it, and are capable of doing worthwhile things with it. It flows through the fingers and flees from people who do not understand it or who do not appreciate it.

Money gives you choices and enables you to live your life the way you want to live it. It opens doors for you that would have been closed in its absence. However, just as with anything, an obsession with money can be hurtful. If a person becomes so preoccupied with money that the person loses sight of the fact that money is merely a medium of exchange that is to be used to purchase things, which can make you happy for a while, then money can become a harmful thing.

Attachment to money will always create insecurity, no matter how much money you may have in the bank. It is a symbol of life energy and if we hoard money—since it is life energy—we will stop its circulation back into our lives. In order to keep that energy coming to us, we have to keep the energy circulating. Like a river, money must keep flowing, otherwise it begins to stagnate, to clog, to suffocate and strangle its own life force. Circulation keeps it alive and vital. This is in line with the law of success of giving and then receiving.

There are many people whose net worth runs from hundreds to billions of dollars. So does this mean that they are very wealthy? A lot of very rich people in the world have no connection with their humanity, and feel very empty with no peace of mind.

Having nice things can provide pleasure, but what is the real meaning of being rich and wealthy? You cannot put a price tag on feeling happy, at peace and content with your life.

Albert Einstein said it well, "Not everything that can be counted, counts, and not everything that counts can be counted." The choice is yours. There is more to life than money.

The truth is money cannot buy everything. For example, money cannot buy peace of mind, good friends, a close-knit family, good karma, work-life balance, time to relax, a worry-free day, good health, quality time with your kids, a new beginning, natural beauty, happy memories, to name just a few. Many people are actually poor because the only thing they have is money.

The second person to die in Spain due to Covid-19 was Antonio Vieira Monteiro, the chairman of Spain's largest bank, Santander. He died alone, in hospital, at the age of 73. However, what was most notable was some words from his daughter's statement, "We are a wealthy family, but my father passed away alone, suffocating, looking for something free, which is air. The money stayed at home." Yes the money stays at home. The bottom line is, that for which you struggle throughout your life that costs you so much time, energy and trouble—in a word, money—really will not be able to help you, when you need help the most.

So having money is only one form of wealth. Money alone does not define being wealthy. Listed below are different forms of wealth, which are equally important, and to live a balanced, peaceful, successful and happy life and create an increase in wealth, you also need to pay attention to the different forms of wealth listed below. Focus on elevating all the different areas of wealth and you will have lasting peace, happiness and contentment in your life.

Health is Wealth

Unless you are healthy, it will be a struggle to be successful and happy. Once you lose your health, you lose everything. It does not matter how much money you have, you spend the rest of your life trying to recuperate your health. Health includes physical, mental, psychological and emotional.

Health, energy and peace of mind are as important to your success and happiness as anything else in life.

When Dalai Lama was asked what surprised him most, he said, "Man. Because he sacrifices his health in order to make money. Then he sacrifices money to recuperate his health. And then he is so anxious about the future that he does not enjoy the present; the result being that he does not live in the present or future; he lives as if he is never going to die, and then dies having never really lived."

To be healthy, one needs to eat well, drink at least 8 glasses of water a day, meditate and exercise, sleep and rest, have regular checkups with your dentist and doctor, enjoy life and do fun activities to regenerate. If you use your brain all week long, you should take one full day where you do not do anything that taxes your brain in any way. Treat it like a muscle that needs a rest after a workout. When you discipline yourself to take off one full day per week from brainwork, you will find yourself vastly more productive during the other six days. You will not miss a thing.

Regular exercise will not only improve your health, it will make you think clearly, boost creativity and manage the relentless stress that dominates our lives. It will add more jest to your life, but it could also add years to your life. Few investments will yield a better return than time spent on physical fitness. Those who do not make time for exercise must eventually make time for illness.

Practise forgiveness. Forgive others who may have hurt you in the past and forgive yourself for any mistakes that you may have made in the past. By forgiving others or yourself, you are actually letting go of the hurt and pain that you are carrying on yourself, which greatly improves your emotional health. You are actually letting go of the past so that you can be in the present moment and it allows you to live longer, happier and a fuller life. The past is gone, the future is not here yet, this moment is a gift, and that is why we call it the "present."

Clear your mind of all clutter and negative chatter. It will keep you mentally fit. 95% of your emotions are determined by the way you talk to yourself throughout the day. With positive self-talk, you can build your self-confidence and self-esteem. For example, when you are given a new and challenging task to do, your positive self-talk or your thought would be "I can do it, I can do it." This will give you the confidence to tackle the task and if needed you will ask for help, and once the task is successfully completed, it will increase your self-confidence, self-esteem and at the same time, you feel mentally good and fit.

Another way to keep mentally fit and healthy is continually associating with other positive, happy and successful people. Get around positive people. Associate with the winners. There is a saying that you cannot fly with the eagles if you continue to scratch with the turkeys.

Feed your mind with positive and uplifting conversations and programs, and attend seminars where you will meet optimistic, ambitious people. Organize your life so that your environment is happy, healthy and uplifting.

Have positive health habits. Your body is a chemical factory, which runs efficiently, based on the foods you put in. It is important that you eat nutritiously, get regular exercise and structure your life so that you get sufficient rest and relaxation. The better you take care of your overall health, the more positive and energetic you are. The more cheerful and optimistic you will feel, and the higher your self-esteem and self-confidence will be. The longer you can work, the more you can get done which makes you feel more and more like a winner in every part of your life.

Have positive expectations for yourself and for others around you. Happy successful people have an attitude of positive expectancy. They expect to be successful in advance. They look for the good in every person and in every situation. Their attitude of positive expectancy translates into a positive mental attitude that affects other people and attracts their support and business. Feeling mentally fit will change your entire personality. You will become a positive, effective, more optimistic and cheerful person. You will get more done faster and easier. You will have high levels of physical and mental energy and, like the Energizer Bunny; you will just keep going and going and going.

Family and Social Wealth

Spending time with your loved ones, having conversations with them and making them laugh, enjoying great trips with them and just connecting as human beings with your favourite people, that is wealth.

When your family life is happy, you will perform better at work. No one gets to the end of their life and regrets making their family a primary priority. They are the only ones who are unconditionally at your side, no matter what. At the time of death, practically only your family members are around you.

In my home, we try to have the family dinner together. My children studied internationally so most of the year were not at home, but when they were, they make it a point to come home in time for dinner. We all enjoy the interesting conversations that happen over at the dinner table. "A family that eats together stays together."

Your greatest treasures will always be the people you love and the people who love you. If you had a short time to live, you would find that your relationships are more important to you than anything else is in the world. All other material things would drop away in comparison to the most important people in your life.

Related to this you also need to forge deep connections with friends and members of your personal community, role models and trusted advisors. The most important and respected people in every community are continually involved in the activities of that community. They join business organizations, support charities, sit on boards, in every way contribute, give back something of themselves to improving the quality of their communities, and in the process create strong lasting bonds and relationships.

Bryan Dysan, CEO of Coca-Cola after working for forty years in the corporate world, was sharing his experience in a speech he made where he said, "Imagine life as a game in which you are juggling some five balls in the air. You name them work, family, health, friends and spirit. And you are keeping all of these in the air.

You will soon understand that work is a rubber ball. If you drop it, it will bounce back. However, the other four balls – family, health, friends and spirit – are made of glass. If you drop one of these, they will be irrevocably scuffed, marked, nicked, damaged or even shattered. They will never be the same. You must understand that and strive for balance in your life."

So get to work on time, work effectively during your working hours and get back to your family on time. Take care of your work, which is important, but at the same time take care of family, health, friends and your own spirit and dreams to live a balanced life.

Having healthy relationships with family and friends enables you to have a rich and successful life where you create memories that last forever.

Inner Wealth

It starts with loving and respecting yourself. This includes a positive mindset, high self-respect, internal peace and a strong spiritual connection. It also includes clarity around your values and beliefs. The more calm, confident, optimistic and positive you are about yourself and your life, the better and higher will be your levels of health and energy in everything you do.

Having a positive mindset means you have positive thoughts and beliefs. In order to create wealth you need to believe that you can be wealthy. If you do not have much money or good health now and your mindset is such that you believe that you cannot have money or have good health then no matter how hard you try, you will never have more money or good health. However, with a positive mindset, even though you do not have much money or good health now but believe you can have a lot of money and good health, then you will certainly do so. This is the power of positive thinking and is a great asset and form of inner wealth to have. You can achieve and have whatever you want. So be conscious about what you are feeding your mind and always think positive.

Career Wealth

Getting to greatness in your profession brings a feeling of satisfaction on a job well done. Being good in your work is also good for your self-respect. Any business you are in, you have to serve and satisfy your customer. Without a customer, there is no business. Customers are the people who use what you produce, whatever your position. If you are an accountant, the financial statements you produce are your product, and your customers are the people who need them and use them to make business decisions.

Career wealth is getting up in the morning, going to work, and saying, here is my chance to provide value and delight my customer. Your ability to identify your primary customer and satisfy him or her at the highest level is the key to your success. Be the best and give more than 100%. Go the extra mile. You have to be different. Do not follow the crowd. It will only take you to places where others want to go. Give more first and the future will take care of itself. When you start a little earlier, work a little harder and stay a little later, you start to give yourself a decisive advantage. You need not need to worry about the returns and benefits. They will just follow.

Your success and your career will be in direct proportion to what you do after you have done what you are expected to do. When you throw your whole heart into the work, you will open up possibilities for yourself that today you cannot imagine. Based on the universal law of success, what you give out, you get back. You will become one of the most valuable and important people in your organization or in any organization. In addition, your future will become unlimited.

Circle of Influence

You become who you spend your time with, so choose your network carefully. If you want to be happy, spend time with happy people. If you want to be successful, spend time with successful people. You will adopt their beliefs and self-esteem.

On the other hand, avoid negative toxic people. Their association will affect your mindset and performance negatively. Get away from them. Do not let them drag you down with their negative, pessimistic attitudes towards life and its possibilities.

Michelle Obama says walk away from "friendships" that make you feel small and insecure and seek out people who inspire you and support you.

Impact Wealth

The deepest longing for a human heart is to know that you are living out the rest of your life providing service to humanity, making a difference in the world helping people and being kind. We do not often think about that, but it is a great form of wealth, and it is a great form of richness.

Adventure and Fun Wealth

The human brain craves novelty and challenge is necessary for our growth and happiness. We become rich when every day becomes an adventure. Meeting new people, visiting new places and going to Broadway shows and art galleries, trying new restaurants and foods will bring fun and joy and enrich our lives.

Many people put all their energy into just one area. The most common choice is work, because work best assuages our survival fears of not having enough and not being enough. Other people become obsessed with relationships and love. Putting all focus on one area does not work. Happiness comes from living and enjoying a full life.

Now that you understand how to create an increase in wealth in all different areas of your life, in the next chapter, I will talk to you about meditation and how it can help you to experience bliss, live and enjoy a life full of peace, happiness, contentment, wealth and success.

Chapter 5
Meditation & Energy

"Sleep is the best meditation."
— Dalai Lama

Each of us searches for good health, happiness, prosperity, knowledge, overall peace and harmony at all times. We strive hard to achieve this state. Is this possible to achieve? The answer is yes, by understanding cosmic energy, meditation and self-knowledge. We need to understand: Who are we? Why are we here? What do we need to do while we are here? And where do we go from here?

Cosmic Energy

Cosmic energy exists everywhere in the cosmos. It is the bond between the stars, galaxies, planets and is the space between each and every one of us. It is the bond, which keeps the entire cosmos in order. It is the life force, maintains order in our life, and expands our consciousness. It is the base for all of our actions and functions.

We receive some cosmic energy while in deep sleep and while being in silence, and some from the foods we eat. It is used in our day-to-day activities of our mind and body, i.e. seeing, thinking, speaking and all our actions. The energy we get while sleeping and from digestion is not enough to carry out all the actions. That is why we feel tired, exhausted and tensed. This leads to mental stress and all kinds of illnesses. The only way to overcome this is through receiving more and more cosmic or universal energy.

Abundant cosmic or universal energy is obtained only through meditation. Sleep is unconscious meditation, and meditation is conscious sleep. In sleep we get limited energy; in meditation we get abundant energy. This energy enhances the power of our mind and intellect. It opens the doors of our sixth sense and beyond. With this boosted energy, we will be relaxed, happy and healthy. It also helps to reach physical heights of our realms.

Meditation is a technique used for thousands of years to develop awareness of the present moment. It can involve practices to sharpen focus and attention, connect to the body and breath, develop acceptance of difficult emotions, and even alter consciousness. Its been shown to offer a number of physical and psychological benefits like stress reduction and improved immunity in the midst of busy schedules and demanding lives that we lead. Meditation does not belong to any particular religion or faith, and is practised in cultures all over the world to create a sense of peace, calm and inner harmony.

Some popular meditation practices are:

Mindfulness meditation. Mindfulness meditation originates from Buddhist teachings, and is the most popular and researched form of meditation in the West. You pay attention to your thoughts as they pass through your mind without judging them or becoming involved with them. You simply observe and take note of any patterns. This practice combines concentration with awareness. You may find it helpful to focus on an object or your breath while you observe any bodily sensations, thoughts, or feelings.

Focused meditation. Focused meditation involves concentration using any of the five senses, and is ideal for anyone who wants to sharpen their focus and attention. For example, you can focus on something internal, like your breath, or you can bring in external influences to help focus your attention such as counting rosary beads, listening to a gong or counting your breaths. This practice may be simple in theory, but it can be difficult for beginners to hold their focus for longer than a few minutes at first. If your mind does wander, simply come back to the practice and refocus.

Movement meditation. Although most people think of yoga when they hear movement meditation, this practice may include walking, qi gong, tai chi, gardening or other gentle forms of movement. This is an active form of meditation where the movement guides you into a deeper connection with your body and the present moment. Movement meditation is good for people who find peace in action and want to develop body awareness.

Mantra meditation. This type of meditation uses a repetitive sound to clear the mind. It can be a word, phrase, or sound, one of the most common being "AUM." Your mantra can be spoken loudly or quietly. After chanting the mantra for some time, you'll be more alert and in tune with your environment. This allows you to experience deeper levels of awareness. Some people enjoy mantra meditation because they find it easier to focus on a word than on their breath. Others enjoy feeling the vibration of the sound in their body.

Loving-kindness meditation. Loving-kindness meditation is used to strengthen feelings of compassion, kindness, and acceptance toward oneself and others. It typically involves opening the mind to receive love from others and then sending well wishes to loved ones, friends, acquaintances, and all living beings. Because this type of meditation is intended to promote compassion and kindness, it may be ideal for those holding feelings of anger or resentment

Visualization meditation. Visualization meditation is a technique focused on enhancing feelings of relaxation, peace, and calmness by visualizing positive scenes, images, or figures. This practice involves imagining a scene vividly and using all five senses to add as much detail as possible. It can also involve holding a beloved or honored figure in mind with the intention of embodying their qualities. Another form of visualization meditation involves imagining yourself succeeding at specific goals, which is intended to increase focus and motivation. Many people use visualization meditation to boost their mood, reduce stress levels, and promote inner peace.

Progressive relaxation. Also known as body scan meditation, progressive relaxation is a practice aimed at reducing tension in the body and promoting relaxation and often used to relieve stress and unwind before bedtime. Oftentimes, this form of meditation involves slowly tightening and relaxing one muscle group at a time throughout the body. In some cases, it may also encourage you to imagine a gentle wave flowing through your body to help release any tension.

For the past twenty-five years I have been practicing aumkar meditation, which is mantra meditation together with 5 healing exercises. It was put together by Dada Bhagwat, who ever since 1945 has been working to find out the reasons of unhappiness in families/instability in society in general, and the solution to these problems. He was guided by Sai Baba, the Saint of Shirdi, that in order to understand the root causes of these problems, he had to understand 'what is human life?' The study must start from the origin of cells to understand the gravity and complexity of solutions. Dada studied human life in detail, including how humans came into being, which includes all the stages from unicellular organism to the stage of humankind. He then designed the meditation to provide maximum benefit, right up to the cellular level, to anyone who practises it. It involves directly connecting with nature and is aligned with the laws of nature. The magnetic field of all possibilities and infinite creativity within you will connect to the magnetic field of all possibilities and infinite creativity in nature, and you will get whatever you want in life as long as you comply with the Laws of Success, Nature or the Universe.

Who are we?

Evolution Theory

During the creation of the Universe, a big explosion took place called the Big Bang by some scientists. It is also known as AUM and denoted as the symbol ॐ. It is at this stage that a part was separated from the whole. An entity was created from Infinity. The first life, the unicellular organism formed by a combination of certain gases and under certain conditions, began in the water and lived by the law of nature and survival of the fittest. Over time the soul evolved into different life forms on the earth and in the air and finally into the human life form (Charles Darwin's Theory of Evolution).This process takes millions of years. In each of the life forms, the purpose of life is for the benefit of others. For example, through the processes of eating and reproducing, an earthworm produces a liquid which is a great fertilizer. Its entire life is spent producing this liquid, and through the earthworm's movement in the soil, it arrogates the soil, making it very fertile.

The first man-in-the-making was the formation of the primitive man living in the caves. These caveman were nearing perfection in structural form but needed improvement in formation and use of super-sensory organs along with quality brain. Here the living pattern started changing from muscle-strength man to mental-strength man. At every stage, an improved human emerged with sensitive and super-sensitive organs and glands. To control various functions of sensitive and super-sensitive nerves and glands, and to ensure proper and smooth daily living, a suitably qualified brain was a **must**. Therefore, the brain also developed simultaneously and acquired a fine memory-membrane which performs the most delicate and intricate functions within a fraction of a second, at speeds beyond imagination. We normally claim this as a reflex action, but this superfine quality of various actions needs appreciation of the wonderful mechanism, which performs so efficiently. It compels us to bow before nature!

At this point starts the effort-based stage of the process of **progressive expansion,** where nature has no role to play, as a suitable physical body has been already provided. It is man and man alone who has to try to attain higher stages in life and living. The only thing mankind has to do is to know in details about those faculty organs contained in their body. On knowing about those organs, human has to use those quality-organs in an appropriate manner so that higher-level results (experiences) are obtained. Progressive expansion is a continuous process in the gross body, which consists of the physical body, subtle body and the casual body and is made up of nineteen elements.

In nature, there exists five elements, which are in the following proportions:

Earth -1: Water - 3: Fire - Infinity: Air - 21: Ether - 108

In nature, balance is always maintained amongst these elements. Any imbalance means great turmoil in nature. As the human is part of the same nature and comes from the same source of creation, the above elements also exist in the human body in the same proportions, and any imbalance amongst these elements causes illness.

Aumkar in Humans and in Nature

The word universe means *one song*. Uni means one and verse means song. Aum is a sound and the song is Aumkar. It exists in nature and formed the first word in creation and origin of speech. It is the field of formless cosmic energy and holds together the atoms of the world and heavens.

Your body is full of Aum. You are the universe and the universe is in you. As shown below, the symbol Aum engulfs the sun, the earth and the moon.

The sound Aum produces a wave as shown below. Our DNA also shows similar waves which shows our body is full of Aumkar.

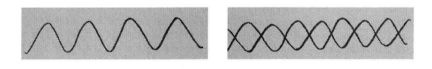

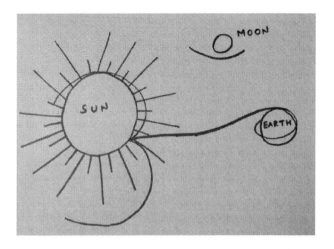

Micro Analysis – We are same as the universe. In our body, energy is the soul. Soul represents the sun, the navel point represents the earth and the forehead represents the moon. In order to live a peaceful balanced life, our body should be in tune with the nature. The elements in our body are in the same proportions as in the universe and they need to be in balance with nature. Earth -1: Water - 3: Fire - Infinity: Air - 21: Ether - 108.

The Human Body

The human body is made up of 19 elements:

Physical Body - 5 Performing bodies
Nose - Power of Procreation
Tongue - Power of Excretion
Eyes - Power of Movement
Skin - Power of Grasp
Ears - Power of Speech

5 Sensory /Supersensitive organs
Earth - Odour - 1
Water - Taste - 3 times of Earth
Fire - Form - Infinity
Air - Touch - 21 times of Water
Ether/Space - Sound - 108 times of Air

Subtle Body – 5 Sheaths or Energy Centers

- **AnandmayaKosh** - Crown Chakra - pineal gland not related to any element - violet colour
- **VidhyanmayaKosh** - Third Eye - pituitary gland not related to any element - indigo colour
- **ManomayaKosh** - Throat Chakra – thyroid gland related to ether/space element - blue colour

- **PranmayaKosh** - Heart Chakra – thymus gland related to air element - green colour
- **AnnamayaKosh** - Solar Plexus – pancreas (navel point) - related to fire element - yellow colour

Casual Body - 4 Existing but non-existent super sensitive organs.

- Intelligence
- Mind
- Genius (thinking mind)
- Nearness to the creator - Microcosm, Macrocosm

The Creator has graciously given these 19 elements as a gift, without our having to ask for them. So out of gratitude, it becomes one's duty to respect and fully develop these 19 elements to the fullest, and achieve the highest ideal life and have peace, happiness and contentment. In general though, everyone in life only uses 7 of these elements: earth, water, fire, air and ether, (physical body) and solar plexus chakra (at the navel point) for digestion of food and the heart chakra for breathing (subtle body).

The remaining elements i.e. the throat chakra, the third eye and the crown chakra, which are responsible for higher thinking, are not used and therefore do not get fully developed. Intelligence and genius have been given to everybody, yet they remain inactive and, instead of experiencing the peace and happiness, which is everyone's right as it has been freely given by nature, one will start to look for it externally in the environment. However, it is all within you; you just need to understand and have knowledge about your own body and use what nature has given and develop it fully to experience the highest ideal life. You can achieve this by doing Aumkar meditation.

Aumkar Meditation

This meditation uses all 15 elements—physical body and subtle body which results in activating the casual body—your intelligence, mind, genius and gives you a shape to achieve the highest ideal life where you become one with nature (microcosm becomes one with macrocosm) and you will start to find all answers within you. Aumkar is universal and not tied to any specific religion. It exists in nature, and since humans come from the same source, it is naturally within our bodies as well. By tuning the Aumkar within you to the Aumkar existing in the nature, you get aligned with nature and can live a balanced life.

Do Aumkar meditation using all the 15 elements, breathing correctly and saying the Aumkar sound using the correct pulse, rhythm and tempo; tune into the Aumkar sound already present in nature and around you. By breathing and saying the Aumkar sound correctly, you automatically have to use all the 15 elements. The 5 elements in your body will combine with the 5 elements in the nature. The meditation is so designed that you are totally aligned with the laws of success mentioned in chapter 2. You will tap into your consciousness, give out good Aumkar vibrations and through the law of giving and receiving you will receive good vibrations. This will make you feel happy so you carry out good actions, creating good karma, and this in turn will help you achieve your intentions and desires. You will discover your purpose in life and work passionately to achieve this purpose and live an ideal life. This way you are achieving your goals effortlessly, making you very happy and content with life.

Aumkar meditation can be done sitting cross-legged on the ground or sitting on a chair. Choose the way that allows your spine to be straight and is comfortable for you.

There are eight steps to the meditation. The following 2 steps lead to the main transformation within you. Please go to my website for the remaining six steps.

Aum – say 21 times, 5 seconds each.

To say the Aumkar, start by inhaling a full breath. Then as the breath is released, the Aum sound is expressed and gradually taken to the point of its pitch and thereafter fades out at the end of the breath. This is 5 seconds long. (Go to my website, which has a recording of the correct way to say the Aumkar sound.)

NYAS Exercise

5 exercises in total, 5 times each while saying Aum – 10 seconds each.

Use your hands and move them while saying the Aum as follows:

- From top of forehead to heart point.
- From back of neck to navel point
- From back of shoulder blades to heart point.
- From lower back to tail bone
- From hip joints to end of toes.

The meditation is a specialized technique, and best learned from a qualified instructor; it cannot be learned from a book. The Aumkar sound produced has to be the same as the Aumkar sound present in the nature to get the actual benefit from the nature; otherwise the effort is wasted.

For the 5 NYAS exercises do each step / exercise 5 times with each Aum 10 seconds long. (shown below). Using the palm of your hands slowly move them as shown in the diagram while saying the Aumkar. For the last step if you are doing the meditation sitting on a chair then just move the palms of your hands from the hips to the knees. Do not bend to touch the toes; you will cut the flow of cosmic energy you are receiving from the nature. This method of infusing Aumkar energy into various parts of the body using the palms of your hands energizes the 5 energy centres or chakras of your body.

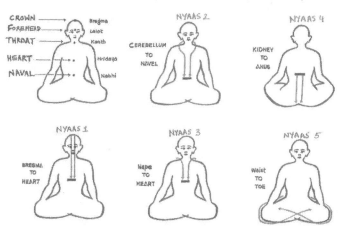

Go to my website to download a full page colour, ready to print copy.

When you say Aum in the correct way for 5 seconds, the sound hits a point in the cosmos, and combines with the five elements earth, water, fire, air and ether present in the atmosphere. This creates an explosion (similar concept to atomic fusion theory) releasing energy which will return back to the point of origin which is you. The original sound wave is now converted to a light wave. This energy or light wave is at a higher speed than the rhythm of your heartbeat. Before you start the next Aum, you breathe in for 3.5 seconds, creating a pause between the two Aums. This pause, if done correctly, will allow the beat of your body to align with the speed of the energy, which is returning to you.

The energy will enter your body through the breath you take and the sweat pores on the skin. The heat from the fire element will evaporate the water contained in the cytoplasm of your cells, which will be eliminated out of the body as sweat through the sweat pores, and the vacuum created by the evaporation of water will be occupied by the energy, which has entered your body and thus energizes you. The energy will be stored at energy centres that you can draw upon when in need. Thus through meditation, your portion of the actoplasm (air + ether) will slowly increase, and the portion of cytoplasm (earth + water) will slowly decrease, enabling you to develop a thick layer of good deeds, which you may enjoy in the future. You will feel very happy and joyful; you will be working with nature, how life has been designed, and you will receive creative ideas and solutions from nature. You become one with nature. It is self-experience only that can help you to understand what I have just described.

Now that we have knowledge of who we are, in the next chapter I will talk about the impacts that the meditation and NYAS have on us. We will also discover why we are here; in other words, the purpose why we took birth so that we can work towards fulfilling our purpose in life. Finally, where are you going from here?

Chapter 6
Purpose

*"Our prime purpose in this life is to help others.
And if you can'thelp them, at least don't hurt them."*
— Dalai Lama

The Soul

When we take birth, i.e. the soul, which is a sublime conscious energy force, needs proper coverage to contain the high-grade energy radiated by it. This has high vibrational frequency. It cannot come on the earth by itself. It has to take shelter, and needs some special coverage to contain the sublime-conscious force so that the 'energy' can be safe in body-haven and allow the soul to activate all delicate and intricate organs in the body. Nature has done this by giving it a human body, i.e. the soul is a spiritual being living in a physical body. This is similar to the supply of electric current. The main grid is stored with very high voltage capacity. Its lower voltage current is supplied to cities. Further reduced voltage current is supplied to transformers on a particular street. Still further reduced capacity is supplied to society and our houses. The current used for the computer or the fridge in our homes is very low, but it is still using the same current as is in the grid.

Similarly, the soul is our grid and the last stored energy is the mind. The mind functions as the medium of the soul which is the main source of energy. It is dormant and needs to be activated. As per medical science we say that a baby is born and never that a soul is born. The body therefore dominates all our activities in life and the soul remains neglected and occupies least importance while living a life, whilst it is actually the main source of energy. This is why I mentioned in chapter 5 that we need self-knowledge and the ability to understand our body so that we can use all the resources that we have been given freely by nature to live a fully balanced and ideal life. The soul takes up a human body as a covering and comes to life to either fulfill a purpose and carry out some decided duties, enjoy and fulfill their karma's or break the circle of lives.

The soul has high vibrational frequency as it comes from higher atmospheric spheres where there is air and ether, which together is called actoplasm. The mind being the medium of the soul, knows what purpose the soul wants to achieve by taking birth. These higher atmospheric layers are listed as well as shown below:

1. Earth
2. Earth Bound Spirits
3. Exosphere
4. Thermosphere
5. Lonoshere
6. (Transformation Stage)
7. Mesophere
8. Strathosphere.
9. (Transformation Stage)
10. Troposphere
11. Lonospheres

Hierarchy of Spheres

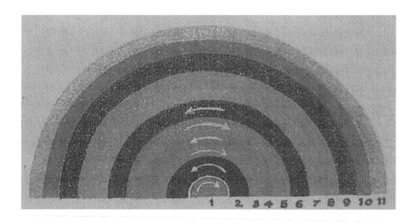

Each sphere is at a higher vibrational frequency, and to move through each sphere requires either clockwise or anti-clockwise movement as shown by the arrows. There are clockwise movements on Earth, anti-clockwise on Earth Bound Spirits, clockwise on Exosphere, anti-clockwise on Thermosphere, clockwise on Lonosphere and so on. As people advance to higher frequencies, they move up to higher spheres. An analogy would be similar to corporate hierarchy in a company. For example, in the accounting world an associate who gets more education and experience will advance to the Financial Analyst position and then to Senior Financial Analyst and from there to Manager, Director and then to Vice-President, CFO, CEO and so on.

Why are you here?

Actoplasm

When you are born, you come from the higher spheres and therefore you have 100% actoplasm, which is a combination of air and ether elements. Then you are guided by the soul as the soul operates under the air and ether elements, and due to the actoplasm you are full of bliss and happiness. Because of the high content of actoplasm, babies are always happy and in bliss as long as they are fed and are comfortable. The higher content of actoplasm makes one very happy, and it also means that they are not in fear.

Actoplasm activates the mind and intellect, and allows the communication between the soul, the body, the brain and the intellect. Then everything works in coordination, and that is why babies achieve so much in their first year of life. They start to crawl, walk and talk, usually single words and a few sentences. Taking the first steps to start walking without fearing that it will fall is a big accomplishment for the baby. As the baby starts growing, it starts losing its actoplasm content, which is replaced by cytoplasm—made up of earth and water, the elements responsible for your desire to enjoy life and the want for material things. The initial cell content composed of air and ether (actoplasm) starts to get replaced by water and earth (cytoplasm). This explains the higher rate of achievement in the 1st year when one is born, as compared to later years as the levels of actoplasm get diminished. Actoplasm is responsible for manifesting your desires into reality. It is the magnetic field around you which combines with the magnetic field of nature, and it attracts into your life whatever you want.

Between the ages of 3 and 5 the baby is already possessive about its toys and the things it wants. It already starts being materialistic, and you will frequently hear a baby say 'this is my toy, I will not share it.' By the age of eighteen or even earlier there is only 25% actoplasm left in the cells and 75% of the body is occupied by cytoplasm, which as mentioned above is a combination of earth and water elements. This will cause the material desires to increase in the body, the body will not get the full development of the 19 elements as well as the speech required to communicate with the soul, and one will forget the purpose and the reason why they have taken life.

Therefore, it becomes important during this period of between 3 to about 18 years to inculcate the mind of the child with fair knowledge about good manners, discipline, health, habits, helping, respecting others and being compassionate, so that a greater portion of actoplasm can be retained which can benefit them in the future. It is an impressionable age and important from the future point of view of the child. Actoplasm manifests your desires into reality. The higher the actoplasm content in childhood, the more easily the child will be able to manifest his or her goals and dreams effortlessly.

Service to Others

Actoplasm makes one feel happy and good, doing good deeds, being kind and forgiving, joyful and in bliss, whereas cytoplasm makes one think materially, i.e. having power, being competitive, greedy, selfish, etc. When you are happy and feel joyful, you are vibrating at a higher frequency. When you are sad or angry you are operating at a lower frequency.

We live in a materialistic society, but in order to live, one must have a minimum of at least 25% Actoplasm. When we make sure to utilize 50% of our lives for ourself and family, and 50% for others, then we will enjoy perpetual happiness. Living life with full knowledge and proper utilization of body is an indication of approaching towards self-realization and living an ideal life.

The human being has received five sensory organs: eyes, nose, ears, tongue and skin. Out of these five the skin is extremely sensitive and a very important organ. It is composed of seven layers of cells, and each layer has a specific function.

The Aumkar meditation and the "NYAS" are closely related to this function, and hence it is important to understand how these sensations are received and sent forward through the nerves to the spinal cord and from the spinal cord to the brain, and how they are analysed in the brain.

Once they reach the spinal cord, they ascend upwards through tracts known as spinothalamic tracts, crossing the whole spinal cord, then medulla oblongata, pons, midbrain and finally relayed to thalamus. Thalamus is an extremely important part in the brain. It is connected by nerve fibres to the sensory cortex, motor cortex, cerebellum and the hypothalamus, the basal nuclei. All these centres have fine communications with each other.

The hypothalamus controls the pituitary gland by stimulating or inhibiting hormones, and the pituitary gland controls the other glands of the endocrine system. When you do Aumkar meditation, you are receiving Aumkar vibrations, (divine cosmic energy) which helps to regulate the hypothalamus and thereby regulate various body functions that are controlled by the hypothalamus. It brings equilibrium in the functions of all centres of the brain. It is self-experience, which can enable you to understand what Aumkar is in reality; and you need to do the meditation to experience it. All these complex things are represented diagrammatically below and simplified for understanding.

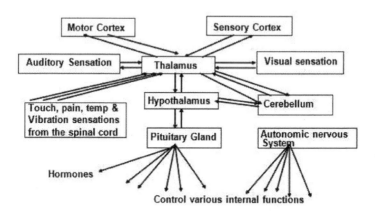

Discover Your Purpose

When you do the Aumkar meditation with your full body, speech and mind, and remain in that vibration for 24 hours, your actoplasm is activated, and starts to increase to a level of 75%. The pituitary gland in the body will start to release messages from the soul. The body and the soul start to communicate and you will be able to intuitively know the reason why you are born, i.e. the purpose of your life and what you need to do to fulfill your purpose on this earth. It is extremely important to know the purpose why you took birth and then work on fulfilling that purpose; otherwise your life is wasted. You came to life for some purpose and you need to complete this before going back.

You can have different purposes based on what stage you are at in your life. By profession, I am an accountant but at this stage of my life, my purpose is as follows:

- Great Teacher
- Great Mother
- Great Artist

It is nothing big like some leaders such as Mother Teresa, whose purpose was to help the poor of India. It took me a long time to figure out my purpose, but at this time in my life, this is what I need to work on. During my life, I got many teaching opportunities and taught in high school, at the University of Concordia in the B.Comm program, coaching for the CMA Entrance exam, moderated for the 2 year CMA professional program, taught meditation etc. I loved it and did it for a short while, but had to stop as I had other priorities. By identifying my purpose, I realize I have a gap to fill my purpose as a great teacher and by writing this book; it is my attempt to start filling this gap.

For my other purpose, I put my children first and drop everything if they need me, and I need to continue on this journey in my lifetime to earn their love. Often I get caught into the busy life between home and work but having 'Great Mother' as a purpose pulls me back to what is important in my life. My children have grown quickly and are adults now, but I keep reminding myself that they are the small miracles that happened in my life. The truth is I am a work-in-progress and I will continue to work on this purpose throughout my life so that at the end of my life I can smile and be happy to be remembered by my children as a 'Great Mother.'

As well, I have seen and experienced many different things in my life, and my lawyer friend in Montreal once commented to me that these experiences are unique to myself and not generally experienced by others. I usually do not talk about these experiences but know intuitively that the medium to express this is through art. I have dabbled at it a little in the past but not done much. I need to work at this and will restart the art classes I had stopped as I was too busy to continue at that time. I hope one day that I will be able to portray these experiences through art and share it with other people.

There are other ways to uncover what your purpose in life is at any given time.

Passion: What are you passionate about? What do you love to do, and when you are doing it, you lose track of time and can continue working on it for hours without feeling tired or exhausted? Working on that one thing actually energizes you. You do not feel that you are working but instead having fun. This then is your purpose in life. There are some people who are fortunate to work on what they are passionate about and get paid for it; for example, Tiger Woods is passionate about golf and he gets paid for playing (work) while having fun. He is using his unique talents playing golf to do a service to humanity by entertaining them and making them happy while creating an abundance of wealth in his own life and having fun at the same time.

Legacy: What mark do you want to leave on this world when you are no longer here? How you live your life will reflect the legacy you leave behind. Initially in life we all strive for achievement and struggle to get respect, usually in the form of material possessions and prestige, but eventually we realize that something is missing. Then we start to think what gift we wish to leave the world when we are no longer here. How we want to be remembered once we are gone. What impact we had on people or places. Reflect on what you want to be remembered for, or the gifts you want to leave behind. Once you identify the legacy you want to leave behind, this then is your purpose in life and you can start working on building your legacy today, not ten years from today. We often think we will have more time, but as we all know that time will never arrive. Identifying your purpose and working on it will help you live a fulfilled life and avoid feeling regret, disappointment and sadness about what could have been when you reach the end of your life.

Where do we go from here?

Travels of the Soul

When a person dies, its soul remains cocooned by webs of desires and wishes if these were not completed during the lifetime. Since desires and wishes are related to earthly pleasures, these are governed by gravitational forces and hence exert downward pressure on the bodiless soul. The natural tendency of the soul is to go upwards towards the higher atmospheric spheres from where it came to the transformation stage, but it is instead it is pulled down towards Earth by the gravitational forces.

It remains stuck between the earth and the transformation stage in a zone known as Earth Bound Spirits or Black Zone. It cannot proceed further on its journey until theses desires and wishes are completed. It is estimated that currently the population of these souls who remain in this hung state is at least 5 to 6 times higher than the actual living population on this earth.

While doing Aumkar meditation, the vibrations created during the meditation with the sound Aum will create clockwise and anti-clockwise circular movements in your body. These will help to cleanse away impurities and your unfavourable karmas. A good analogy would be the laundry washing machine with its clockwise and anti-clockwise movements scrubbing and removing dirt from the clothes. As you regularly continue with the Aumkar meditation, the soul gets tuned in with the clockwise and anti-clockwise movements so that when it leaves the earth, it uses these movements it has been accustomed to propel itself and move forward in the exosphere, thermosphere and Ionosphere zones to get to the transformation stage or green zone.

By doing the Aumkar meditation on a regular basis you increase the % of actoplasm in your body, which has the tendency to release the good vibrations into the atmosphere. It can expand out from your body (your aura). The good vibrations created will help the others around you who may not be feeling well or are sad, and in this way, indirectly, you are providing a service to others by making them feel better. The other benefit by doing meditation is you will be using all of the 15 elements that have been provided by nature and will activate the other 4 from their dormant state to an active state. This means that you will be living a full-elevated life using your intellect, mind and genius, and achieving many successes.

Therefore, by the end of one's life they will no longer have any wishes or desires because whatever they wished for, they will be able to acquire it during their lifetime with the help of their mind, intellect and genius and the higher content of actoplasm in their bodies. It will be a fulfilled, satisfied life and when it is time to leave the earth, the gravitational pull will not be strong to keep the soul downwards towards the earth.

Instead, because of the higher amounts of actoplasm, it will be the etheric force which will pull the soul upwards towards the higher atmospheric spheres, making its way up to the transformation stage. Additional benefit while doing the Aumkar meditation, the body gets accustomed to and familiar with the clockwise and anti-clockwise movements and now it can easily travel in the exosphere, thermoshere and Ionosphere without any difficulty, and quickly reach the transformation stage within 10 to 12 years.

The time taken by Law of Nature for those who have not been exposed to the clockwise and anti-clockwise movements, and who do not have enough actoplasm but have plenty of desires and wishes which remain unfulfilled, is 360 years to traverse from the earth to the transformation stage. What a difference in timing between 10-12 years and about 360 years.

From a personal development perspective, it is important to think about the legacy you want to leave behind, and live your life accordingly. But it is even more important to prepare yourself and fulfill all your wishes and desires and have a high level of actoplasm so that you can proceed on straight to the green or transformation stage and birth zone without any obstacles. Nobody will be there to help at that time, so it is very important to prepare for that journey now. No use repenting after.

It should be noted that these states can be achieved not only through meditation, but also by living a purposeful life providing service to others, doing good deeds, spreading universal love, giving charity and showing kindness, which will all increase actoplasm. For example, a doctor provides a service to people who are sick, showing them kindness and helping them to heal and get better. One may say that they get paid well for it, but payment or compensation is a different subject matter, which is based on the quality of the service they provide and how easy it is to replace them. Scientists, musicians, artists etc, come to provide something very specific to the earth.

Leonardo Da Vinci came to earth to provide some great paintings. Saints come to provide happiness and peace. These people give something very unique to the world or provide a great service and hence have a lot of actoplasm.

The present life is therefore very important. You have to identify your purpose, fulfill it and be of service to others to achieve your highest ideal life. Even for corporations, corporate service responsibility (CSR) is a very important activity and employees or members of the organization are encouraged to participate in CSR activities. The more you give and be of service to others, the more you receive. In the next chapter, I will talk about learning, and how important it is to learn every day and grab every opportunity you get to learn to achieve your goals and be successful.

Chapter 7
Learn, Learn, and Learn More

"Learning never exhausts the mind."
— Leonardo da Vinci

Keep Up With Change

In chapter 1, I talked about the importance of learning. From the time you take your first lesson in elementary school until the time you pass on, you are a lifelong student. You never stop learning. You learn something new every day.

People who have more information have a tremendous advantage over people who do not. And though you may think it takes years to acquire the knowledge to be successful, the truth is that simple behaviours such as reading for an hour a day, turning commute or television time into learning time, attending classes and training programs can make it surprisingly easy to increase your knowledge— and substantially your level of success.

In the digital economy, you learn and study as if your entire future depends on it, because it does. As you move at hyper speed into the digital arena and the information age, your ability to learn and apply new ideas and skills is the absolute prerequisite for your success. Knowledge and know-how are the keys to the 21st century. In addition, the more you learn, the more you earn.

It is a challenge to keep up with this mind-boggling explosion of knowledge, but it is certainly possible to learn and increase your knowledge every month in some way. There are various sources for learning and education. There is a lot information available on the thousands of free websites on the internet.

Various Ways to Learn

Schools, Colleges & University

This is the traditional and formal way of getting educated, and the degrees and diplomas awarded will enable people to get better jobs, earn more and succeed in life. The formal education prepares you to prepare and write tests and exams on regular basis to move forward. You learn how to analyse information, create solutions, make decisions and then implement them depending on the discipline you are studying.

For example, a medical student will learn how the human body works, and what happens when some interactions taking place in the body break down, and what treatment will work to heal the body. They will then provide the correct medication or, if an operation is required, refer the patient to the appropriate surgeon or specialist.

By the same token, an accounting student will learn the accounting principles and standards and how to apply them to recognize revenue and match the appropriate expenses to earn profit, or how to calculate the return they are making on the investments, and then decide and implement those opportunities which provide the necessary return on investment.

The graduates from these institutes have a higher probability of being employed in the field that they studied. They know the subject matter theoretically and have been tested and examined on it, and with some coaching and training will be able to put it into practice on the job in the real world.

So get a formal education. It is your insurance that you will be employed. If you work and put your full heart into it, you will have a solid chance to have a successful life.

Continuing Education and on-line learning

Many institutions offer courses whereby you can obtain a full degree on a part-time basis. You can also take short courses which may have a short duration of maybe a month or up to six months, which will allow you to learn about a subject matter very quickly, or get a refresher on a subject you have studied a few years before. You can be working and studying at the same time. For example, a person can take a securities course to learn how the stock market works, and study about different companies and how they are doing on the market, and then use the learning and the information to invest in stocks and make money on the side while working at their regular job at the same time. Another example is learn about real estate and then use the learning and information to invest in properties and make money on the side as well.

When you study a particular subject, you never know when in the future this knowledge will come in handy and change the course of your life.

Steve Jobs dropped out of Reed College, but the college offered the best calligraphy instruction in the country. Throughout the college, every poster, every label on every drawer was beautifully calligraphed. Because he had dropped out, he did not have to take normal classes and so Steve decided to learn calligraphy. He learned about serif and sans-serif typefaces, about varying the amount of space between letter combinations, about what makes great typography great. It was beautiful, historical, and artistically subtle in a way that science cannot capture, and Steve found it fascinating. There was no hope of a practical application in his life at this time, but ten years later when they were designing the first Macintosh computer, it all came back to him, and he and his team designed it all in the Mac. It was the first computer with beautiful typography. If he had never dropped in on that single course in college, then the Mac would never have had multiple typefaces and proportionally spaced fonts; and since Windows just copied the Mac, it is likely that no personal computer would have them either.

Learn to connect the dots – be a Leader

Continuing with the Steve Jobs example, if he had never dropped out, then he would never have dropped in on that calligraphy class and personal computers might not have the wonderful topography that they do. Of course it was impossible to connect the dots forward when he was in college but it was very, very clear looking backwards ten years later. Again, you cannot connect the dots looking forward. You can only connect looking backwards. Therefore, you have to learn to trust the fact that the dots will somehow connect in your future. You have to trust in something, your gut, destiny, life, karma whatever, because believing that the dots will connect down the road will give you the confidence to follow your heart and your passion, even when it leads you off the well-worn path. That will make all the difference. Do not follow the crowds; be a leader and create your own path to follow.

Learn by reading

In chapter 3, I wrote about books providing a connection to the outside world. At a fraction of the cost, books allow you to get knowledge about the rest of the world and have great conversations with an author. They will enable you to learn how they think, and about their success strategies. Books also allow you to recognize your own talents, and build your confidence and self-discipline.

Successful people read a lot. Many of them read a book every week, which means 52 books in a year, 520 books in ten years, and over a thousand books in twenty years. It's easy to become a top expert in your field and have an edge that others simply don't have. After reading a book, review what you have read and apply at least one thing that you learn from each book, and you will be miles ahead of everyone else in creating an extraordinary life. In addition, you can read on any subject. I came across a trucker's magazine and I just started flipping through it. By the time I finished, I had learned about things that I had never thought of before, and came to understand many of the challenges that this industry faces.

You can even take a course to learn to read faster so that you can absorb the information faster. Reading biographies and autobiographies of great people provides you with insights to become great yourself.

Learn from your mistakes

To err is to be human. There is nothing wrong with making a mistake. We are human. Mistakes offer us a powerful way to learn and grow. Just do not make the same mistake more than once. Otherwise, you miss the important lesson that is available to you, which suggests that you are not paying attention and listening to life.

Each day life sends you chances to learn, grow and become your best. Do not miss these opportunities. Some opportunities never come again, and you will regret not taking the opportunity. If you do not try, you will never know. Richard Branson said, "If somebody offers you an amazing opportunity, but you are not sure you can do it, say yes— then learn how to do it later."

Attend conferences and retreats

These provide powerful learning experiences, and additionally beneficial is the excitement and inspiration of your fellow attendees and the networking that goes on at these events.

Learn by teaching

When you learn something, teach it to somebody else to reinforce the learning. It is the fastest way to clearly understand the new material, and you see the process from the eyes of the teacher. Often, this activates the "doer" in you. If you cannot find someone to teach it to, then take out a blank piece of paper and teach it to yourself. It helps to solidify the subject matter in your mind.

Learn from a good movie

Happy Feet
The children's movie "Happy Feet" is all about penguins trying to fit in, and finding your purpose. From birth, Mumble the penguin was different. Instead of singing, he tap-dances. That is right. A tap-dancing penguin. All Mumble wants is to belong, but his peers harass him constantly. He is always disappointing his father, Memphis. Every time Mumble tap-dances, Memphis scolds him: "It just isn't penguin, okay?" From the start, the movie is about self-expression, and how individuality is one's most important gift to society. "Happy Feet" supports individuality and showcases the discrimination against those who do not or cannot conform. "Happy Feet" has also other lessons to teach us, about family, love, friendship, and standing up to bullies. It teaches us that it is okay to be different.

Long Walk to Freedom
The movie "Long Walk to Freedom" chronicles the life of Nelson Mandela, from the time he was a naïve young lawyer focused on his own success to his evolution into the legend he eventually became.

The legend's journey had something in it for everyone, but more so, for anyone who is trying to create something out of nothing, who is trying to create a change in society, much like what Mandela did.

Some Invaluable Lessons

1. Celebrate the small victories. Mandela was convicted of inciting people to strike against apartheid, and was sentenced to life imprisonment. One of the first things that happened after he was taken to the Robben Island prison was the handing out of the prison uniforms. The Blacks were handed shorts while the others were handed trousers. Mandela and his band of comrades protested against this small injustice over the next few years. This period was marked by violence by the Afrikaner guards, intense physical labour, and almost inhuman conditions in the 8x7 foot cell. However, they never gave up their demands for the same prison uniforms as the Afrikaners. So finally, when the full-length trousers were given a few years later, the band of prisoners erupted in joy, clapping and thumping the prison walls, to celebrate their small but undeniable victory. As an entrepreneur, businessperson or an employee, daily life can be exhausting, with small setbacks seemingly amplified by our minds. It is important to celebrate the small milestones—a big client sign-up, a certain number of users reached, or even a colleague's birthday. This can boost morale and set you up for the next few days.

2. Learn to let go. During the course of his 28 years in prison, Mandela watched helplessly as life passed him by outside the barbed wires. His mother passed away and his first-born son, who he was very attached to, was killed in a road accident and despite his requests to attend the funeral, he was not allowed to do so. Two of his most loved ones in the world passed away and he could neither save them nor be at their bedside in the last few moments. In a heartbreaking scene in the movie, he receives the letter informing him of his son's death as he is toiling in the scorching sun in the prison courtyard. He breaks down, weeps out of helplessness, and then carries on living. One day at a time.

Similarly as an entrepreneur, businessperson or employee, there are things you can control, and then there are things that are out of your control. You cannot change the mind of a customer who cancels the contract at the invoicing stage; you cannot change the mind of an employee who decides to quit your start-up or your company and takes up a cushy corporate job somewhere else; let it go. Look at the things you can control—they need your attention desperately.

3. The organization is bigger than an individual is. As Mandela and his comrades entered middle age in prison, South Africa was burning. Anti-apartheid protests and violence was spreading. Not just violence by the Blacks against the ruling Afrikaner, but also violence within various communities of Blacks. When a fresh group of young prisoners was brought into the Robben Island prison and they saw Mandela tending to his beloved tomato garden, one of the revolutionaries erupted in anger—"You are tending to your tomatoes while the rest of South Africa is burning." Mandela's response was simple—"Alone, you can accomplish very little. But together, the African National Congress

(ANC) can bring about change." He was not swept up in emotion, but retained his strong belief that sustainable change can be brought about only by the ANC.

4. Having a vision is not enough – sell it! During the last few years of Mandela's prison life, the Afrikaners realized that they could not 'rule' over the Blacks anymore. Therefore, they started involving Mandela in talks with various ministries on the way ahead. His wife Winnie Mandela thought he was 'selling out' to the Afrikaners by talking to them; his own comrades, who had been loyal to him for decades, thought that they might assassinate him or corrupt him; practically no one supported him. However, his vision was clear–to bring about lasting peace, with the one unshakeable tenet being that all people be treated equally, that the Blacks seeking revenge against the Afrikaners for centuries of atrocities would not be the solution. Therefore, he went ahead, selling his vision to his colleagues and the Afrikaner ministers alike. This was his greatest achievement, perhaps even surpassing his nearly three decades spent in prison in protest against racism. As entrepreneurs or businesspeople, we need to sell ourselves every day, at every occasion provided. That is probably the single biggest sales opportunity that is underused by many of us.

5. Let your experiences make you better, not bitter. Nelson's wife Winnie was his partner in every sense of the word. While he was in prison, she experienced untold miseries. Being constantly picked up from her home by the cops for 'interrogation,' beaten up, kept away from her young daughters, and once even kept in captivity without trial for 16 months–she had an equally tough life outside. As the years went by, lives took different trajectories. Winnie became bitter, angry and hostile against the Afrikaners, inciting the party members to extreme violence, putting the social fabric at risk. Nelson sought lasting solutions, not just revenge. They finally parted ways, with Nelson taking control of the ANC and saying that he still loved the Winnie he fell in love with, not the person she had become. The fact remains that a huge majority of start-ups fail. If your start-up fails, it might seem like there is not even a trace of the dream for which you gave away years of your life. But that is not the case. The start-up makes you grow as a human, and gain invaluable wisdom and life lessons. Who would want to trade that away for anything? Get better, not bitter—no matter the outcome of your start-up or situation.

Learn From Covid-19

For years, we have been encouraged to be isolated, as in caring only about ourselves, focusing only on our own well-being, which we are told is solely in our own hands. We have been encouraged to think of ourselves as islands, and that our health, happiness and prosperity are independent of the larger community, society or country, never mind the world. It is unfortunate that it takes something like Covid-19 to convince us hopefully once and for all, that as human beings, we can never be independent of each other, and our health, well-being and prosperity is very much in each other's hands. Twenty years from now, we will look back and say, "thank goodness for this coronavirus." What we are witnessing is the beginning of a complete and far-reaching restructuring of life, business and communication. Covid-19 has removed 80% of the vehicles from the streets in a manner that no environmental adult activist could. It has removed

90% of the people from buses, trains and subways. This is as good a time as any to reflect and think carefully about what our priorities should be in the future. Covid-19 gives us an opportunity to learn and break away from business as usual. It gives us the ability to embrace new paths, more sensible paths. A possible path that could see us reducing vehicular emissions. The curse of this coronavirus becomes a blessing for those who would use this opportunity to be courageous. Coronavirus is a test run for global warming. Mother Nature is showing us what we are capable of, and what kinds of actions we have to take in extreme situations. Now that we have learnt from the pandemic and virus, we can use the knowledge to fight global warming.

After learning from Covid-19 that as human beings, we can never be independent of each other, and our health, well-being and prosperity is very much in each other's hands, I will talk in the next chapter about relationships, and investing in others to live a healthy, happy, prosperous and successful life.

Chapter 8
Invest in Others

"Nothing is perfect. Life is messy. Relationships are complex.
Outcomes are uncertain. People are irrational."
— Hugh Mackay

Correlation to Happiness

The primary aim for anyone in life is to achieve happiness. Every goal that a person strives for leads to another goal and then another, and then another until the individual arrives at the final goal. And the final goal is always happiness. For example, you want a better job. Why? So that you can earn more money? Why? So that you can buy a bigger house, a better car and improve your family life. Why? And the final answer is always because you feel that will make you most happy. When you are happy and full of joy, you are operating at a higher vibrational energy. As per the principle "Like attracts Like" you will begin to attract more things into your life which are also vibrating at a higher frequency, making you even more happy.

Almost 85% of your happiness will be determined by your relationships with other people. It is how well you get along with others, and how well they get along with you, that will determine your level of happiness and satisfaction in life more than any other single factor. Relationships are central to a successful life. They are everything. If you accomplish all your material goals, but you do not attend carefully to your relationships, you will end up empty, alone and miserable. However, if you have wonderful relationships with people who care about you, and whom you care about, then no matter what happens in the outside world, you will be happy and successful.

We are all social creatures and we all crave friendships and positive interactions. The better our relationships, the happier and more productive we are going to be. There is no other skill that will do more to assure you of great success, achievement and satisfaction in life than to be extremely competent in getting along with other people. Therefore, it is necessary to invest your time in people and engaging in certain behaviours that can dramatically increase your effectiveness and influence with other people and build lasting, happy relationships. Below are the foundations of all happy relationships.

Never criticize, condemn or complain about other people. Look for the good in others rather than criticizing. Discipline yourself to look for the solution to a problem rather than complaining about it. Take, for example, someone who is going through some problems and is hurting inside, but did not mean to yell at you. Even though you have done nothing wrong, the solution to this is not yelling back. Then there will be a conflict and there is no difference between you and that person. You will feel anger and you will start operating at the lower frequency and be at the same level as that person. Instead, be emphatic, show compassion, and be positive, supportive and uplifting. Send good thoughts, hoping everything is fine with the person. This way your feelings and emotions remain at the high frequency that you were operating at and you will avoid the other person's emotions affecting you. The relationship remains intact and the other person will realize what they have done. Therefore do not condemn other people for their behaviours but rather, realize that in similar circumstances, you might behave the same way. If you cannot say something nice, do not say anything at all.

Be agreeable. Agreeable people are welcome everywhere, and the way to become agreeable is to refrain from disagreeing or challenging other people. Be tactful and diplomatic in your relationships with others. Everybody hates to be told that they are wrong, and when a person says or does something that is obviously incorrect, whenever possible let it go. If a person is disagreeable with you, turn the tables by being pleasant and agreeable with them. Everybody wants to be right. When you allow people to be wrong without saying anything, it puts you in a position of greater power and influence in the situation.

Practise acceptance. We all want to be accepted for exactly who we are. Unconditional love and acceptance of your spouse, your children, your friends and co-workers is one of the most powerful relationship tools. This can be done simply by smiling. When you smile at another person, openly and genuinely, you express complete acceptance of that other person in that instant, and they feel happier inside and their self-esteem goes up. In turn, you will feel happier yourself and your self-esteem goes up as well. You will start feeling relaxed, positive, cheerful and optimistic. And all it costs is a simple smile.

Appreciation. Whenever you appreciate anyone for anything, they feel happier, more valuable and respected. You cannot appreciate people too much and too often. This can be done simply by saying the two words "Thank You" on every occasion. Appreciation satisfies one of the deepest needs of all people. You can thank people for small things as well as large things. You can thank your children for helping around the house, or your team for completing an assignment on time. Use "thank you" on a regular basis.

Admiration. Everybody likes a compliment. You can admire the quality, traits or possessions of other people. You can admire a person for being thoughtful, punctual, or generous. You can admire the clothes, car, home or possessions of other people. When you find something about another person that is worthy of admiration, and comment on it, the quality of your relationship with the person will improve immediately.

Quality of approval. This satisfies the deepest craving of human nature, the desire to feel important. Praise people for their accomplishments, small and large, for their progress even if they have not yet achieved the desired result. When children are praised by their parents or teachers, their energy levels actually increase. When adults are praised for any reason, they feel more positive and more energized. Approval causes a person's self-esteem to go up immediately. One of the keys to effective praising is for you to do it immediately after the action. The faster that you praise a person for something they have done, the more impact the praise has on their personality. When you praise people for a particular behaviour, it makes them feel so happy about themselves that they are much more likely to repeat that behaviour as soon as possible so that they can earn even more praise. They like themselves more and they like you more, as well.

Pay attention. Pay careful attention and listen when people talk to you. It is one of the most wonderful ways to build the self-esteem in the other person to cement the quality of your relationship. Listen attentively without interruption or saying something to stop the train of thought. Face the person directly and watch their mouth and eyes as they speak. Lean forward, nod and approve as a person speaks. Intently listening to what the other person is saying, taking a pause before replying, and asking a question for clarifying and paraphrasing will show the person that you really value them, and is a very efficient way of working with other people, especially in the world of work. When people are intently listened to by others, their blood pressure increases, their heart rate goes up, their self-esteem improves and they feel happier overall. And you can achieve all of these things with another person by merely stopping everything else that you are doing and listening very intently to whatever it is they are saying.

Benefits of Having Good Relationships

1. Physical needs. There are many immediate benefits to forming and maintaining excellent relationships. However, there are long-term benefits as well. The quality of your relationships will largely determine how long you will live, and how well you will live during that time. Each person has a series of needs that must be fulfilled for him or her to be happy and healthy. The first of these are physical needs, and your ability to communicate and interact with others is so important that the absence of quality relationships can jeopardize and even shorten your life. People who live alone or who are socially isolated are two or three times more likely to die prematurely than those with strong relationships. The more problems one has with their relationships, at any age, the more likely they are to be sick from a variety of causes.

2. Intrapersonal & interpersonal skills. Intrapersonal skills is defined as how well you get along with yourself. It is how well you know yourself, understand yourself, are clear about your strengths and weaknesses, your values, opinions, goals and dreams. You are then self-aware, and this will allow you to be honest and objective with yourself, and as a result, you are more honest and objective with others as well. Interpersonal skills is the ability to communicate, negotiate, interact, persuade and influence other people. You need to have both intrapersonal as well interpersonal skills to be successful in all businesses requiring active interaction with other people to have productive outcomes. A higher degree of ability to get along with a greater number of people will do more to improve the overall quality of your life than perhaps any other skill you could develop. You will get more work done.

3. Networking. It is another type of business relationship where the number of people you know and the number of people who know you in a favourable way will determine the amount of success you achieve in life. All successful people know many other successful people. They go out of their way to create business associations and then contribute to each other's successes and provide each other useful help and advice. Mutually beneficial relationships are established which are very useful over time.

4. Personality and character. In every instance, it is the quality of your personality and your character that is going to have the greatest effect on how well you get along with other people and how open and willing they are to helping you achieve your goals. The perfection of character is the ultimate aim of human life. There are certain parts of your personality that will remain completely untouched or undeveloped unless and until you enter into deep, meaningful, intimate and emotional relationships with people you love and who love you in return.

The experience of bringing children into this world, raising them and lavishing your love upon your children with no expectation of return or appreciation before they reach adulthood, requires that you reach deep into yourself for depths of feeling that you never knew existed before. It is these great emotional riches and breadth of personality that makes you a more interesting and complete individual. It is hardly possible for a person to become everything they are capable of becoming without the lessons and understanding that come through relationships with people for whom we care deeply and who, in turn, care for us deeply as well. The purpose of existence is not to make a living but to make a life—the perfection of the character.

5. Level of self-esteem. Your level of self-esteem, i.e. how much you like yourself, is the critical measure of how healthy you are as a human being. It determines your levels of energy, enthusiasm, self-confidence, happiness, peace of mind and your overall personal performance. The more you like and respect yourself, the better you do at everything you attempt. In fact, everything you do in life is either to protect or to increase your self-esteem. The quality of your relationships is absolutely critical to your level of self-esteem. When you are getting along wonderfully with other people, you feel terrific and your self-esteem will go up. When you are getting along poorly with other people, you feel negative, anxious and insecure.

6. Social needs. We all have three basic social needs, which are inclusion, control and affection. Each of us needs to feel included by others, both socially and at work. We need to feel that we are part of something bigger than ourselves. We need to feel wanted, accepted, useful and important. We are happy to the degree to which we feel we have a certain amount of control over our lives. Most stress and unhappiness is caused by a feeling of being out of control in some parts of our lives that are important to us. We also have a desire for affection, a desire to care for others and to know that they care for us. It is hard to live without knowing that someone cares about us. Building and maintaining quality relationships is extremely important to satisfy our social needs.

Relationships may be extremely complicated way down deep, but to build and maintain quality relationships only requires a few simple concepts:

Trust. All relationships are based on trust. As long as the trust is there, the relationship can go on indefinitely. To build trust, you always keep your word. You remain consistent and dependable in everything you say and do. You behave as the kind of person who is utterly reliable in every situation.

Respect. Take the time to express your respect for the uniqueness, specialness and differences of the other person, which makes her or him, feel very valuable and important. When you treat their values, opinions, goals and dreams with the same respect that you would like them to treat yours, you build and enhance the quality of your relationship.

Caring. There is nothing that so improves the relationship than for you to genuinely tell the other person that you like them, love them, care about them, and are concerned about their well-being and happiness. The greatest gift you can give to another person is the gift of unconditional love and acceptance. The kindest thing that you can do is to refrain from criticizing, condemning or complaining to them or about them for anything. Catch them doing something right and always look for ways to make people feel more valuable, more respected and more loved in everything you do. The three most powerful words in any language are still "I love you." Repeat these words as often as possible and demonstrate that you feel these words in as many different ways as possible.

Communication. To communicate well with others, time is the critical factor. Relationships can be made to increase in value to both you and the other person, depending on the amount of time that you invest in them. When you take the time to ask the other person how they feel, how their day went, how their life and work is going, you open the channels of communication. And when you are listening attentively, calmly, quietly with total attention, while the other speaks, you improve the quality of your communication. By listening attentively, you demonstrate the respect you have for the other person and you deepen the level of trust between you.

Spend time with your spouse and children uninterrupted every day, after the responsibilities of the day have been taken care of. The more time you invest in the important people in your life, the more important and stronger those relationships will become. And the better your relationships are, the happier you will be. You both benefit enormously.

Courtesy. When you say "please" and "thank you" on a regular basis to the people in your life you make them feel better about themselves and about what they are doing. Do not be rude to the people whom you care about the most. Emmett Fox said, "If you must be rude, be rude to strangers and save your manners for your family."

Praise and appreciation. Praise and appreciate the other person for everything that he does or she does, both small and large. When you express your appreciation for another person or something they do for you, they not only feel better about themselves, but they want to do more of it. And every time that you thank or appreciate another person, your own self-esteem goes up. When you praise someone for their efforts, even when they are not successful, their self-esteem goes up measurably. They feel stronger, happier and healthier about themselves.

Helpfulness. Provide help wherever you can. Your constant willingness to step in and do little things for others is always appreciated and respected. Willingness to share, to contribute, to help each other out, is an important part of the foundation of lasting relationships.

The most important ingredient for a long, happy, healthy life is a sense of balance between your work and your relationships. No success in public life can compensate for failure in the home. It is absolutely essential that you plan and organize your time in such a way that you spend ample time with the important people in your life. Your relationships must be central, not peripheral to your work. Learn and practise every tool of time management so that you can get your work done in the time allotted so that you can spend the evenings and weekends with the people, you care about the most. Ask yourself on a regular basis what you would do if you only had six months to live. How would you change your life and how would you spend your time? I think that you will find that your material considerations, which involve you totally during most of your day, will shrink to insignificance if you thought that you only had a short time left. Your relationships would instantly become paramount in your existence.

The most important rule regarding life and personal relationships is this: "It is quantity of time at home and quality of time at work that counts." And you cannot mix them up. Family and your relationships require high quantities of unbroken chunks of time that allow you to walk, talk, communicate and interact without pressure or stress. They cannot survive on so-called quality time. Work on the other hand requires quality time, working on your highest-value tasks and concentrating on them single-mindedly until they are complete.

You can have a wonderful life, live to a long age and be a completely happy and fulfilled person by putting your relationships first, and everything else second. First work on yourself and decide what it is that is really important to you, then go to work on your relationships and become the kind of person who is really important in the lives of others.

Perhaps the most important thing that you ever do in life is to build and maintain long-term happy, healthy, fulfilling relationships with other people you love and who love you. When you make everything else secondary to this central purpose, you will find yourself enjoying happiness and rewards out of all proportion to the effort that you put in.

In the next chapter, I will talk about foods that you eat which makes you further feel healthy and very good. Feeling happy and good impacts your work life, your personal life and your relationships.

Chapter 9
Food

"Food for the body is not enough.
There must be food for the soul."
— Dorothy Day

You Are What You Eat

The general saying goes you are what you eat. Your diet is everything. Making the right food choices goes a long way towards protecting your brain and your health. Your health, energy and peace of mind are as important to your success and happiness as anything else in your life. Earlier in chapter four, I mentioned that health is wealth. If you lose your health, then no matter how successful you are, nothing is more important anymore and no matter how much money you spend, you cannot buy your health back. Food has a very big influence on the health you enjoy.

Eating the right foods can affect your physical, mental and emotional health. Regular practice of following these simple ideas below can enable you to live longer and enjoy your life:

Maintain proper weight to have high levels of energy and be physically fit. If you consume more calories than you burn up through exercise and daily activities, you will store the extra food in the form of fat. So eat less and burn more calories than you consume, change the proportion of the foods you eat, and the times of the day at which you eat them. Make lunch the biggest meal of your day; it is best to eat lunch around noon as the digestive fire within you is at its brightest at this time and allows for efficient digestion. Have dinner around 6.00 p.m. This should be a smaller meal than lunch as you are no longer active at night. Your body will feel more settled and comfortable when it does not have to digest full rations at night.

You also need to think differently about food. Your mental picture of seeing yourself as healthy, fit, slim and trim will make you think about how you feel after you have eaten, and you will stop eating once you have satisfied your appetite to feel lighter and leaner, rather than eat more and feel heavier and fatter. It will help you to choose healthier foods.

Eat more fruits and vegetables, which are packed with vitamins, minerals, antioxidants and fibre, and are also lower in calories. One needs about 50 to 60 grams of protein per day for proper brain and body functioning, which you can easily get from plant foods and whole grains, although you may choose to keep some meat in your diet for taste, social or other reasons, and have some lean source proteins like fish, chicken and eggs. Eat complex carbohydrates that do not spike blood sugar, avoid bad fats and eat more healthy fats, which include monounsaturated fats like olive oil and the anti-inflammatory, high omega-3 fat found in seafood, flax, hemp and chia seeds, avocados etc.

In addition to eating protein and lots of fruits and vegetables, you should drink about eight glasses of water per day, which will keep your entire system flushed out. You will help your body to remove excess salts, sugars, toxins and waste products. One of the best ideas in health is called hydration, meaning you keep your body as full of water as you possibly can.

Lastly, if you want to enjoy high levels of physical fitness and energy you need to reduce sugar and salt. Sugar of any kind, except that from complex carbohydrates such as fruits and vegetables, has a negative effect on your body. It raises your glucose levels and leads to mood swings and depression. As for salt, you get enough salt in your diet and naturally from the foods. Excess salt can raise your blood pressure and lead to hypertension and heart disease.

Food For Your Brain

Our brains rely on a complex symphony of chemicals to keep our moods in check and to function properly. They are equipped to learn new subjects, rise to a challenge, enjoy an exciting adventure, or just relax contently. However, when our brain chemicals get out of whack, all sorts of problems can arise. We can become depressed, unable to concentrate or unable to sleep. We can feel over-the-top ecstatic one minute and completely dispirited the next all because our brains are getting the wrong quantities of chemicals.

The three brain chemicals responsible for thinking and feeling are serotonin, dopamine and cortisol, and the key to feeling better lies in rebalancing these three brain chemicals. Serotonin is responsible for feelings of calm, optimistic and self-confident; dopamine for feeling excited, motivated and energized; cortisol is the stress hormone, which the body uses to switch into high gear to meet your large and small demands. Imbalanced cortisol levels can leave you feeling exhausted, unmotivated and dragged out during the day and sleepless at night. High levels of cortisol can also depress dopamine levels while preventing serotonin from binding to certain areas in your brain and inhibiting neurogenesis—the creation of new brain cells.

What your brain needs

- Proper nutrients, including the right vitamins, essential amino acids, and healthy fats
- Exercise
- Sufficient restful sleep
- Downtime for relaxation and restoration
* Regular healthy circadian rhythms
- Purpose and meaning
- Spiritual practice
- A connection to something larger than yourself

Nutrition is the top on the list for what your brain needs, and by providing your brain with the nutrients it needs, you immediately put yourself on the path to thinking and feeling better. In order to function optimally, your brain needs amino acids, vitamins and omega-3, and just by changing the foods you eat, you can radically change the way you look and feel. The remarkable thing about the brain is that it is designed to balance its own chemistry, provided it gets the right nutrients from the foods you eat and the other supports listed above, such as physical, mental, emotional and spiritual approaches. I am not a medical professional and for any medical issues, you should consult a doctor.

Eating anti-inflammatory foods, folate, vitamin B12, vitamin D and tryptophan can help maintain balance in the brain chemicals and actually improve your mood and sharpen your brain. Blood sugar has a huge bearing on our brain chemistry, and the foods we eat can either produce steady levels of blood sugar, or they can induce sugar rushes and crashes, which can leave us feeling foggy, anxious and depressed. When your blood sugar spikes too often, it breaks havoc in your brain as well as your body. This means that every time you overindulge in too many unhealthy carbs, you are putting yourself at risk of not being able to remember who your significant other or children are in later life.

Energy From Food

The more energy we have, the better we feel. So what eats up our energy? Where is it used up? You will be surprised to know that over 50% of our energy is used up in the digestion of food. We use 35% in doing our regular work, 10% is used up for family, friends, and 5% is left for ourself. That is why we feel very tired and are always looking for ways to increase our energy.

So the more efficiently that you digest food, i.e. the less energy that your body has to spend on digesting, the more energy your body will have to carry out other functions such as removing toxic material from your body. Over time, toxins accumulate at a faster pace when you are not digesting your food efficiently. You have to get rid of these old waste and toxins to allow the digestion to function optimally. Your energy will automatically increase because your body will be able to perform digestive and other functions efficiently and with much less effort, and you will also feel much better.

As the function of digestion takes up the maximum amount of energy, we should be eating foods that assist with digestion and perform it efficiently. So let us take a look at what nature has designed our bodies to eat. In the animal kingdom, there are the herbivores and carnivores. Our genetic makeup is more close to the primates—monkeys, chimpanzees and gorillas. Our teeth, like the monkeys', are flattened except the front canines, which can be used to help open up the harder shells of some fruits. Our back molars are appropriate for grinding plants for easy digestion. Our livers and our stomachs are designed to digest plant foods. Our liver has a low tolerance for uric acid, a by-product of animal protein. Our digestive tract—the human intestine—is extremely complex and at around thirty feet long. It is almost twelve times as long as our torso, similar to a gorilla who also has a long intestine. Nature has designed it to be long so there is adequate time to absorb the minerals and nutrients of fruits and plant matter, which quickly break down and move through our bodies.

On the other hand, the liver of a carnivorous animal such as a cheetah or tiger contains uricase, which is an enzyme used to break down uric acid, giving the cheetah or tiger's liver about fifteen times the capacity to break down uric acid from animal protein than a human liver has. The carnivorous animal also has a short intestine—only about three times the length of its torso. Its intestinal tract is designed for quickly getting rid of the acidic waste matter, which is the by-product of animal protein. So what happens when we have the biological makeup of a gorilla but we eat like a tiger? Trouble, as we are going against the natural laws of biology.

When hunting, carnivorous animals always hunt down and eat herbivores and never another carnivorous animal. This is because they need the chlorophyll from the herbivore's plant-based diet. This confirms that, in the end, it is plant-based food that is required by herbivorous as well as carnivorous animals. Gorillas, elephants, rhinoceros, hippopotamus, giraffes are natural vegetarians and though their plant-based diet is composed mainly of green leaves, shoots, stems, roots, bark, nuts, flowers and fruits from which they get adequate proteins, they are in fact the strongest animals on this earth. Eat fruits and lighter foods first as they require shorter time for digestion and can move along in the intestine without causing a traffic jam—a similar concept to cars and trucks on a road. If a truck is in front of the cars then it creates a traffic jam holding up all the cars. Similarly amongst fruits, eat a melon first as it is mainly water and is digested quickly. It will move faster than a banana, which takes more time to digest than a melon.

Food For Your Body Type

As per the table in chapter 5, our bodies are made up of 5 elements, which are earth, water, fire, air and ether. These elements are a code for shapes of intelligence that make up a person's mind and the world they perceive through that mind.

Earth + Water
Kapha
Phlegm

Water + Fire
Pitta
Wind

Air + Ether
Vata
Bile

Everyone has a unique body type, and living in tune with the nature—easily, comfortably and without strain—meaning respecting your uniqueness.

These are the three main ways in which the elements combine to form the different body types, which are **Kapha** (predominance of earth and water), **Pitta** (predominance of fire and water), and **Vata** (predominance of ether and air). All three body types are present in everyone but when you are conceived, you are programmed with an ideal combination in which one of the body types will predominate. If maintained in balance, that blueprint will ensure vibrant health throughout your life. This always stays the same and becomes your home base. When you are feeling well, it is because the three different body types are in balance with the predominant one in check. This is your state of vibrancy as nature designed it to be as your natural state. It means that your diet, lifestyle and your environment are affecting your body type in a healthy way. Most commonly, people have a single dominant body type. They are either Kapha, Pitta, or Vata. Go to my website at successinthedigitaleconomy.com to determine your body type.

Vata types control movement, are enthusiastic, have a thin physique and a very active mind, learn quickly but also forget quickly.

Pitta types control metabolism, tend to be precise and orderly, become angry or irritable easily, are fond of cold foods and have a sharp intellect and articulate speech.

Kapha types control structure, gain weight easily and lose it more slowly, have a calm disposition, needs eight or more hours of sleep and have very good stamina, physical endurance and steady level of energy.

Every cell in your body has to contain all 3 of these principles. To remain alive, your body has to have Vata, or motion, which allows it to breathe, circulate blood, pass food through the digestive tract, and send nerve impulses to and from the brain. It has to have Pitta, or metabolism, which processes food, air, and water throughout the entire system. It has to have Kapha, or structure, to hold the cells together and form muscle, fat, bone and sinew. Nature needs all three to build a human body.

Vata is cold and dry and therefore the warm nourishing foods like hearty stews and soups, slow cooked casseroles, fresh baked bread, fruit pies and thoroughly cooked foods that are easily digestible create a soothing diet for Vata types.

Pitta is hot, therefore cool and refreshing foods with less salt, oil and spices are best for Pitta types.

Kapha is slow, so light meals for breakfast and dinner, lightly cooked foods, raw fruits and vegetables works well for Kapha types. Spicy foods will promote better digestion and warm the body.

Food For the Subtle Body and the Soul

In chapter 5, I had also mentioned that our gross body is made up of the physical body that we can see; subtle or sensory body also known as energy centres or chakras, which we can't see or touch; and the causal body. The soul also gets hungry, and the food for the soul is meditation and is directly correlated to the causal body.

The subtle body or energy centres/chakras receive, process, express your vital life energy, and allows this to flow through the body. This flow of energy is what creates optimal health and well-being.

Each chakra is also associated with a specific colour. Colour is pure energy, and light is simply the vibration of radiant energy that is visible to our eyes. The seven colours of the rainbow all have varying wavelengths and frequencies. Red is at the lower end of the spectrum and has a lower frequency, while violet is at the top end of the spectrum and has a higher frequency. Adding more of a particular colour to your life—especially by foods of that colour—can have a positive balancing effect and can give a specific vibrational energy boost to the corresponding chakra and the emotions associated with it. Go to my website to see the different colours related to the different chakras.

Root Chakra - Earth Element - Colour Red: related to your most basic survival needs and sense of belonging. Physically it is centred around your hip area and the base of your spine. It governs safety and security, as it relates to foods grown right in the earth, which are the most balancing for this chakra, such as root vegetables—sweet potatoes, red-skinned potatoes, carrots, yam, and all types of squash, ginger, onions, shallots, parsnips and radishes. Seeds, nuts, legumes including lentils are also good in moderate amounts. Since the colour of this chakra is red, all red foods help boost and balance its vibration, including red apples, strawberries, red pears, red cherries, red tomatoes, radishes, red beets, red bell peppers, etc.

Sacral Chakra - Water Element - Colour Orange: holds the energy of your creativity. Physically, the sacral chakra is centered just below your navel, in your lower abdomen. Because the element associated with this chakra is water, hydration is key to keeping movement as an optimum level in your body. Orange is the colour vibration of this chakra, and orange foods include carrots, sweet potatoes, oranges, yams, orange bell peppers, papayas, butternut squash, apricots and peaches, and balance energy in this chakra. The orange colour in foods is present in part because of beta-carotene and the plant carotenoids, which help protect your cells and keep you vibrant and fluid.

Solar Plexus - Element Fire - Colour Yellow: Balanced energy in this chakra gives you the fire, confidence and inspiration to accomplish what you seek to do. Physically this chakra is centred in your gut or solar plexus, which is the area right above your navel. When balanced it radiates motivation and inspiration. Yellow foods such as lemons, spaghetti squash, pineapples, yellow summer squash, yellow bell peppers, quinoa, millet, bananas, yellow pears and yellow apples help balance the energy in this area.

Heart Chakra - Air Element - Colour Green: Energy from this chakra is derived from pure, unconditional love, compassion and empathy. It is anatomically located right in your chest, around the physical heart. Green foods such as spinach, broccoli, kale, chard, romaine, collard greens, mustard greens, arugula, mixed greens, brussels sprouts, green apples, vibrate with this energy, and will help open the heart chakra.

Throat Chakra - Ether Element - Colour Blue: governs self-expression, self-knowledge and communication. It enables us to gain wisdom from our inner truths and experiences. Physically this chakra is centred in the throat area. Foods that are balancing for the energy of this chakra are soups stews, fruits with high water content and sea vegetables such as dulse and nori.

Ajna or Third Eye Chakra - not related to a specific element - Colour Indigo: Third Eye energy is associated with higher intuition, perception, insight, wisdom, dreams. Physically this chakra is located behind the centre of the forehead. Purple/indigo foods such as purple grapes, purple cabbage, blueberries, blackberries, purple kale, purple potatoes and purple plums resonate with vibration of this chakra.

Crown Chakra - not related to a specific element - Colour Violet: The energy of this chakra is associated with filling the unity between oneself, universal energy and a divine presence. It sits on the crown of the head and represents all-encompassing energy. Practising non-attachment to particular foods is a great way to balance this energy.

How You Eat

How you eat is as important as what you eat. We have five senses—see, hear, touch, taste and smell—therefore eating food that tastes good is important and will send a signal to your body of the enjoyment; the other senses also need to send signals that make your body happy; it is the only way to completely make use of the mind-body connection.

Your whole body is tremendously alert while you are eating. Your stomach cells are aware of conversation at the dinner table, and if they hear harsh words, the stomach will knot with distress. Then everything you digest and that meal will be affected, because you have taken in indigestible sounds. Your stomach cells cannot literally hear, but the brain, taking in what the ears hear, sends out chemical messages to update the stomach and every other organ. Therefore, you cannot fool any part of your digestive tract into thinking that a meal is a happy one; your "gut feelings" know better.

A single meal can change the brain's biochemistry quite radically, and serotonin connected with feelings of well-being goes up and down in response to the food being digested in the food tract.

Your body will bubble with joy after every meal if you follow these simple rules:

1. Eat in a settled atmosphere.
2. Always sit down to eat.
3. Never eat when you are upset.
4. Eat only when you feel hungry.
5. Do not talk while chewing your food.
6. Eat freshly cooked meals whenever possible.
8. Eat at a moderate pace, neither too fast nor too slow.
9. Avoid ice-cold foods and drinks. Instead, sip warm water with your meal.
10. Experience all six tastes at every meal (sweet, salty, sour, pungent, astringent, bitter).
11. Leave 1/3 to 1/4 of your stomach empty to aid digestion.
12. Sit quietly for a few minutes after your meal.

Now that you know what foods to eat which are conducive to your physical and subtle body, in the next chapter I will talk about the most important person in your life—Yourself.

Chapter 10
Yourself

"The world as we have created it is a process of our thinking.
It cannot be changed without changing our thinking."
— Albert Einstein

You are the most important person in the world. You are the person that you think about the most and are most concerned about virtually all the time. From your own personal point of view, you are more important than anyone else. How important you think you are determines your character and your personality. The more important you are to yourself, the more important you become to other people. Depending on how much you like, respect and value yourself, your levels of self-esteem and self-respect will increase dramatically and will determine your levels of happiness, health and self-confidence. How important you feel you are also determines the quality of your relationships and your interactions with other people.

Many years ago, I ended up in the emergency department in the LaSalle hospital in Quebec. I underwent surgery the next day and was told that I would not have any children unless I was lucky and was put on strong medication. I was in the hospital for a week, and as I lay in bed in pain, I realized that something had to change in my life. I put everyone else first. I was not a priority. This had to change and I had to put myself first if I wanted to achieve my dreams and goals. Otherwise, I would be very frustrated, end up being very ill, and lose everything.

With the change in my thinking and my belief that I would be a great success, I started taking the necessary actions to achieve my dreams. I started to ignore any obstacles, setbacks or disappointments that came my way. I started focusing on what I wanted to do and stopped worrying about what others were thinking about me or wanted me to do. My life started to change and everything happening to me started to change as well. I learned how to get the results I wanted in any area, and started building more confidence in my ability to get those results, and ultimately achieved the success I desired.

In the airplanes when the plane crew announce the emergency measures, they mention that in the event of an emergency, oxygen masks will be released and asks everyone to put the oxygen mask on themselves first before attending to the children or anyone else. You can only help others if you are well and healthy yourself. You need to think about yourself first and breathe in the oxygen before you can be of real help to the others. You can only bring hope to others if you feel hope for yourself. You can only share wealth with others if you possess wealth yourself. Similarly, you can love others, only if you know what it feels like to be loved. In conclusion, we can only give to others what we possess.

About six months after my surgery, my husband and I went on a cruise to Bermuda. Being at sea, and all the fun and excitement on the cruise ship, did wonders and I started feeling better and recovered from my surgery. Up until then, I had never thought about having children seriously but after being told that I might not have children, this became my priority. I was constantly thinking about children. I started making plans to adopt a child. When I went to the shopping mall, I went to the babies' and children's clothing stores, looking at all the outfits and thinking which outfit I would buy if I had a girl or which one if I had a boy.

With so much of my attention and focus on having children, I was overjoyed to find that I was expecting my first child. It changed my entire life. I considered myself very fortunate and important, and this helped me to set the goals that I wanted to achieve. I persisted by putting in the efforts to achieve them. I wanted to stay at home and raise both my sons. I tried doing this, but found it very difficult to do it full-time. I needed some outside stimulation and thought that if I was in business, then I would be able to make my own hours and work when I wanted and be home with my children when I wanted.

This was the start of our first business, and along the way I realized that having a professional accounting designation with a focus in management would be useful in running the business. Therefore, the next step was enrolling at McGill and Concordia universities, investing in my education completing CMA and MBA executive option. At the same time I bought two more businesses and then moved to a large national telecommunications company to handle bigger areas and responsibilities.

With whatever had happened to me, my purpose in life at the time was to give the best to my children and, over time, it has remained the same. I left jobs because they were not serving my purpose to give the best to my children. By the same token, I also stayed in jobs where I did not want to be, as I needed the money to pay for my children's education. My sons are both in the medical field and studied in

Europe, and we had to pay international fees. Upon their return to Canada, they have had to redo their studies to get the equivalent Canadian degree, studying the same subjects, and we had to pay international fees again.

As I started putting myself first and began investing in myself on all fronts—in my education, my health, the pursuit of my dreams and goals and whatever was important to me—it opened up a whole new world of opportunities for me. I have run and operated my own businesses, lectured at the university in the B.Comm program, coached at the CMA Entrance National Exams, served as a board member on not-for-profit organizations, chaired the audit committee, worked at large, medium and small organizations, spent time helping society, humanity and the environment.

I consider myself a work-in-progress, continuously working to learn, improve and invest in myself following the path that I have always followed—SIMPLIFY.

Along the way I have achieved a lot, and been knocked down more times than I can remember where I had to pick myself up and start all over, but one thing is clear; life is very precious and is a blessing. It is to be enjoyed, I am to be happy and at peace with myself at all times, content with whatever I have, give out happiness and love to the world, and serve and help as many people as I can.

Invest in Yourself

No doubt, the pandemic Covid-19 has effected every one of us around the world and stunned us into silence. We do not know who in our circle of family and friends will be struck next by the virus. We stayed locked up in our homes, not knowing when things will open up and life will be back to normal. However, we cannot let this silence pervade our entire being. There is an opportunity here to learn and take specific actions to emerge from this disturbance transformed as follows:

1. Install some good habits which work for you and follow them through. 95% of everything you do is based on your habits. You can learn new habits that are consistent with the kind of life you want to live and kind of things that you want to accomplish post Covid-19. Once you have locked in a positive habit, you will find it easier and easier to get better and better results in that part of your life. Good habits are hard to form but easy to live with. Bad habits are easy to form but hard to live with. You need to decide upon the habits that are most conducive to your success and happiness, and then work on developing them every single day until they become automatic. If you develop one new habit every quarter, in five years you will have twenty new habits which will bring you all the success and happiness you are looking for, plus all sorts of new opportunities.

2. Learn something new every day. Every moment is an opportunity to learn something new. You can learn formally by attending school, college or university, or in the current digital arena learn online anything that you want. This will improve your thinking, knowledge and skills. Alternatively, you can learn informally by playing with children, observing how they learn, play and interact with other people in their childlike manner, learn from books, movies and even from playing certain games such as "Snakes and Ladders." It is fascinating to see that if you get the correct roll of dice, you can climb up the ladder, in some cases exponentially and equally you can end up on a snake and come down from wherever you are to the starting point. Life is similar, where you can climb a ladder and be high up or can easily come down a snake, but the opportunity to climb up remains and you just need to be patient and take your turn at life again. Learning this way helps to make the journey of life interesting.

All problems contain the seeds of opportunity, and this awareness allows you to take the moment, learn from it and transform it to a better situation or thing. This way, you will have many teachers around you, and many opportunities to evolve and improve yourself, broaden your horizons, eliminate fixed thinking and allow many different people and opportunities to enter into your life.

3. Fulfill your responsibilities and desires. Another way of saying this is to finish your incompletes and do not procrastinate. When you take the responsibility to do something, take the accountability seriously and get it done. It is easier to say "I will take care of it tomorrow." However, that tomorrow never comes and as time goes by, you end up creating a mess, which can rob you of the success you deserve. Every mess is a lock on the gate that keeps abundance out. It could be a physical mess such as your office, garage, basement, clothes closet etc. that is easier to see and fix, or a relationship mess, which is more damaging and harder to resolve. Your desire is to have an organized life where your work life as well as your home life runs smoothly. There is only limited time you have on your hands to carry out your responsibilities, so instead of procrastinating on activities, which may potentially become a mess and bring chaos into your life, identify the activities that you love to do.

For the remaining activities which you do not enjoy doing, find somebody and delegate these activities to them to complete. This way you fulfill your responsibilities and at the same time meet your desire to have an organized work and home life. Every mess you eliminate, no matter how small, brings relief of enormous proportions, and you will feel increased vitality, joy and enjoyment. Now you can focus on only doing what you love and enjoy doing.

4. Invest in your health. Health is wealth. It is your insurance against any serious illness such as cancer, obesity, diabetes etc. Your body is your own temple. So be careful how you treat it and feed it, as it is sacred. Exercise more; walk at least 30 minutes everyday, stretch your body or do yoga for about 15 minutes, do meditation to stimulate and activate your mind. Eat good foods such as a wide variety of fruits and vegetables in season and of every colour. Do not skip meals as you will get hungry and then will reach for junk and unhealthy foods. Drink 8 glasses of water every day to keep your body hydrated and the blood flowing freely throughout your body. Go for outings in the nature to get fresh air and be with nature. The exchange of energy will do you wonders, and the increased oxygen will keep you healthy and feeling young. Spend some time with yourself in silence; reflect on your goals in solitude. Have enough sleep and rest. It will help you to think more clearly, manage stress and boost creativity.

Laughter is the best medicine, so laugh more. When you start laughing, your body chemistry changes, and your chances to experience happiness are much greater. You can laugh from the body or from your mind. Adults tend to judge and evaluate what is funny and laugh from their minds whereas children, who laugh much more than adults, laugh from their body. They laugh all the time that they are playing. Try letting out the child inside you, and play and laugh more.

Being healthy will not only enable you to be productive and take care of yourself, but it will allow you to take care of your family and all the people you love, and live your life more fully.

5. Put family first. When you come on this earth, you are surrounded by family and when it is time to leave, the only people around at the last moment are family. Throughout your journey in life, these are the people with whom you share your moments of happiness or sadness. They are the first people who you want to tell about that promotion you received, that award you won or that goal you scored. They are also the same people with whom you share your failures, that interview you lost or that pain you experience. They stand behind you, sharing your moments of happiness or sadness and providing you with love, comfort and security. Your children are miracles that life has given you to raise. The greatest gift that you can give your family is to spend time with them and let them know that you love them. Put them first wherever you can. Appreciate them, understand them, love them, support them when they need you and help them achieve their dreams. You will never regret it.

6. Plan and set goals to get what you want. As the old adage goes, "What gets planned, gets done. What gets measured gets done." Plan what you want to achieve in one month, one year, 5 years, 10 years, and then write down your goals. Be very clear about what it is that you want and then write it down. By writing it down it becomes real and tangible instead of a vague idea that only resides in your mind. Unwritten goals are just dreams. By writing your goal, you create your own personal roadmap. You have a destination now and know where you want to go. Tony Robbins said setting goals is the first step in turning the invisible into the visible.

The goal has to be a SMART goal:

Specific
Measurable
Attainable
Realistic
Time-bound

E.g., I will lose 10 pounds and weigh 150 pounds by June 15th. This is a specific goal which is measurable, attainable and time-bound i.e. June 15th. It is realistic as I am giving myself 6 months i.e. 2 pounds a month to achieve this goal.

Once the goal has been written, then keep it somewhere visible. This tactic reminds you to keep working on your goal daily. As you are writing down your goals, use a positive tone so you stay excited about completing them. Once the goal has been decided on and is written down, create an action plan to determine how exactly you will meet

151

that goal, and all the steps you need to take to get there. The timeline you have determined will create a sense of urgency, which in turn will motivate you to stay on course and meet your goal. Along the way, measure your progress. Once you see how close the finish line is, you will feel more motivated to push through to the end. If you are a little behind, make the necessary adjustments and keep going.

So setting goals will help you to take action to achieve them. Create goals for every area of your life that you want to improve. When you have a goal, anything is possible, but when you have no goal, nothing is possible.

7. Create great relationships to be happy and have success. 85% of your happiness is determined by your relationships with other people. It is how well you get along with others, and how well they get along with you, that will determine your level of happiness and satisfaction in life. When you are getting along wonderfully with other people, you feel terrific. When you are getting along poorly with other people, you feel negative, anxious and insecure. Relationships are central to a successful life. If you have wonderful relationships with people who care about you, and whom you care about, then no matter what happens in the outside world, you will still be happy and successful. Relationships are like a plant, and need constant care before they bloom. You have to make small consistent gestures such as show understanding; thank, trust and respect people; keep open communications; pay attention; show appreciation and admiration; pay a compliment when warranted; practise acceptance; be agreeable; and do not criticize. This will create and maintain great relationships.

The most underestimated quality, which can help you improve your relationships, is forgiveness. Even though the other person has wronged you, forgiving the person and letting go of the hostility and hatred that you may have bottled up inside you is actually something you do for yourself rather than for the benefit of the other person. When you bear a grudge against someone, it is almost as if you carry the person around on your back with you. He or she drains you of your energy, enthusiasm and peace of mind. However, the moment you forgive the person, you get them off your back and you can then move on with the rest of your life.

8. Give more to get more. Life is like a photocopier. It gives an exact photocopy back to you. Whatever you give out comes back to you. You reap what you sow. Give out good thoughts and goodness to others and the same goodness will return to you. Therefore, to receive more, give out more of what you want in life. If you want more love and appreciation in your life, then give out more love and appreciation to others and it will return to you. If you want more money, then give out more money or help others make more money. If you want more success and happiness, then give out happiness and help others get successful.

9. Find your purpose in Life. Everyone comes to life to fulfill a specific purpose. Princess Diana's purpose was to ban the use of land mines. Mother Teresa's purpose was to help the poor of India. One of US President Abraham Lincoln's purposes was to eliminate slavery. You are here to fulfill a purpose. It is up to you to find what that purpose is. Once you know your purpose then the knowledge of your purpose will lead you to the insight that you are true potentiality.

Through the daily practice of silence, meditation, practice of non-judgement or spending time in nature, your actoplasm increases. This in turn activates the mind and intellect, and allows the communication between the soul, the body, the brain and the intellect. Through this communication, when your brain, soul and mind works together in coordination, you will come to know intuitively the purpose for your life; what you came to achieve in this world and give back to humanity and the world. When you are living your life in this way, you will achieve unlimited abundance as you will be living your life exactly as you had planned to do. This is not temporary abundance; it is permanent, and when you are serving the needs of your fellow human beings with the unique talents you have, you will experience a miraculous life, not occasionally but all the time. You will know true joy and the true meaning of success, and you will create abundance of wealth.

Conclusion

The Covid-19 pandemic has changed our lives in ways we never imagined. For most of us, the changes came so fast we barely had time to adapt. Now, we're at a different stage, depending on where people are. It means that we will have to learn to come out and begin to socialize and be with people more. As more and more people get vaccinated, and with better treatments, there's more herd immunity and fewer people are going to the hospital. The "new normal" is we have to learn to adapt and live with the virus.

Digital transformation has been one of those important buzzwords in recent years, with which we have all become familiar. However, during the pandemic, it really came into its own and several factors contributed to the digital transformation's recent domination. Trends such as an increased dependence on cloud computing, the explosion of data across the organization, artificial intelligence (AI), machine learning, (ML), smart grids and social media, IoT, the next generation 5G networks, mobile web services and the wider need for firms to develop digital platforms—are all driving digital transformation and radically changing the business landscape—reshaping the nature of work, as well as the boundaries and responsibilities of enterprises. These trends go beyond technological innovation.

The pandemic disrupted life on a global scale but as we begin to emerge post-pandemic, businesses will need to plan new business strategies and operations that will limit risk exposure, take advantage of the digital technologies, exploit opportunities presented during the pandemic and adapt to the "new normal."

The digital economy is creating new opportunities for global growth and prosperity. It was always perceived that employees need to be present at work to be productive and be in front of the customer to sell the company's products and services. But the pandemic has proved that if anyone needs to work remotely, they can still be efficient as well as productive. Even the customers have adapted to buying online and do not need someone to be physically present in front of them to buy the company's products or services. Online shopping, teaching and entertainment have taken off in a big way. This new trend where employees can work remotely will create a shift where people live, as they do not have to be physically located close to their workplace. The increased bandwidth and capacities of the networks which are now available due to investments made by companies to improve their networks and infrastructure during the pandemic will allow employees to work from anywhere. This also means that talent can be recruited and hired from anywhere around the globe. All these new learnings which have now emerged post pandemic will shift the way people and organizations organize themselves in the "new normal" and into the future.

Organizations now have the option to let employees work remotely and reduce some of the real estate they are holding and save some of their fixed rental costs. By the same token employees can move out into remote areas where housing and property taxes are cheaper and reduce their personal costs. Or move completely to a warm & tropical place if that's their preference and enjoy this type of weather all year round while working remotely.

In the "new normal" the world has changed in what we do and how we get things done in countless ways. You may wonder what does this have to do with Success in the Digital Economy. With the universal laws of nature or success and with the SIMPLIFY principles? Well, everything.

On March 11th 2020 when the World Health Organization announced the Covid-19 pandemic, nobody knew exactly what to do or what would happen. Suddenly lockdowns were announced in many parts of the world. Nobody had any idea how long that would last or who would be impacted by the Corona virus. It was a scary time for everyone. There was no instructions except to practise social distancing so people turned inwards to humanity and divinity within themselves and started to practise meditation, yoga, going for long walks in the nature and to be in nature more. People started to "give" more, you would often hear stories about people dropping off groceries and food at kerbside, calling on family and friends making sure that they are ok and praying for those who were impacted by the virus. Surviving the pandemic, living a purposeful life and providing service to humanity became the uppermost thought in everyone's mind.

Families, friends, communities, restaurants and organizations got together providing food for lunches and dinners to the front line workers as well as to foodbanks and praying for everyone's safety. As we began to run more digitally, streaming entertainment companies such as Netflix, Amazon Prime Video, Disney Plus etc. added a lot more content and movies for people to watch while they were at home during lockdown. Those who were in the teaching business started offering free online courses to give something for people to do to improve themselves so that once everything was opened they would be ready with new skills. Others offered free online wellness programs, such as aerobic exercise, meditation, yoga etc. to help the people at home to stay healthy.

People became resilient and adapted to whatever came up. They became flexible or agile during this chaotic times. They stayed indoors during lockdowns and curfews when asked, wore masks in public places and even took the vaccines—the first, second and booster shots even though there was not enough testing done or information available on the side effects of the vaccine. Everyone just did what they needed to do to keep themselves, their families and others around them safe. Families and personal life became extremely important. Life is short, and people realize the importance of being healthy, eating well and eat the correct types of food. Eating too much food even if it is very healthy, can cause digestion problems and make people sick. Exercise, meditation, yoga, walking and other practices helped to keep people positive and healthy and to have the Energy to face whatever was happening in the external environment.

With so much good streaming content available, one had to be disciplined and create good habits and manage the time between doing work, entertainment and spending time with family. The positive thinking and energy also helped to take advantage of online learning, so once the chaos starts to subside these individuals will come out ahead with new skills and create more wealth in their lives. With the increased interest in people and making sure they were ok during the pandemic will certainly improve relationships personally as well as at work. The pandemic impacted everybody's life. We were all in it together. As people started to focus on themselves and created improvements in all the different areas in their lives, they started to think about how they could be of service to others and the purpose of their life.

All of the above ways of adaptation to the situation which came up are the SIMPLIFY principles, and they demonstrate that these principles worked in pre-pandemic era, during the pandemic, and will work post-pandemic as well create more wealth and success in people's lives.

Organizations have been equally impacted by the pandemic as well and are adapting to be more agile and similar to individuals, organizations are giving as much importance to customers as well as to their employees. Employee satisfaction is given equal consideration as customer satisfaction. Organizations are surveying their workforce to find out and get the employees input into the design of the new workplace. The health and wellness of employees have taken priority during the pandemic. The employees are encouraged to learn keep their skills up to date so that they can take over more interesting and value added work and be successful as machines, robots and artificial intelligence (AI), starts to play a bigger role in the digital economy and start taking over the routine work. More focus is given to Corporate

Social Responsibility (CSR) activities as employees are asking for this and want to contribute to communities through their companies. And lastly what is the purpose or mission of the organization. The purpose will determine the talent the organization wants to attract. With digitization and ability to work remotely, the employees will have a choice where they want to work and whether the purpose of the company is congruent with their own values. All of the above also demonstrates that the SIMPLIFY principles are equally applicable in the workplace and if followed helps to create wealth and have success in organizations as well.

Manufactured by Amazon.ca
Bolton, ON